Teens: How do y̶͟ you, take you serious., ̶ ̶ ̶ ̶ ̶ ̶ ̶ future? *How to Raise Respectful Parents* is your guide for how to do both.

Parents: Does your teen tune you out? Do you wonder how to communicate so they more easily tune in? *How to Raise Respectful Parents* is your guide to improved teen communication.

How to Raise Respectful Parents is a teen's guide to navigating adult culture by equipping teens with communication skills. Each chapter introduces a new communication skill by using real world examples and conversations between parents and teens. Teens will feel empowered as they try their new communication skills at home, school and work, laying a foundation for entering adulthood. These skills empower teens while enticing parents to read and practice the relationship building and communication skills outlined in the book. Teens will learn how to grow meaningful, more satisfying relationships with their parents through sample conversations and communication exercises about popular teen subjects including homework, driving, friends, dating, social media and more. Tips are also included for helping teens deal with adult culture.

"Teens, this book tells you what you need to know to manage your parents, yourself, and difficult situations with skills that will serve you well throughout your life." —*Sharon R. Carter, Ph.D., Clinical Psychologist, Life and Executive Coach, Pagosa Springs, CO.*

i

"Laura Reagan has produced an excellent guide to assist teens in developing good relationships with parents. She teaches skills that are not only valuable, but can be mastered with practice. She does not avoid difficult scenarios but provides down-to-earth guidance in navigating such situations." —*Chad Richardson, PhD., University of Texas Rio Grande Valley Professor Emeritus of Sociology, Edinburg, TX; Author of Batos, Bolillos, Pochos y Pelados.*

"Through homework hassles and communication issues, Reagan's strategies will help teens and parents build better futures together."—*Susan Valverde, National Supplemental Education Expert, Baltimore, MD.*

"YES! The title declares an under-utilized view and approach in the sphere of family interpersonal dynamics. Teens most definitely have a role in guiding their parents' development. I am grateful my parents were open to this when I was growing up. Thank you, Laura, for this amazing reminder of what's possible when you lead with love."—*Bobby Jasso, Singer-Songwriter/Actor, Los Angeles, CA.*

"This book provides hands-on advice and action steps for teens to create positive relationships with their parents. Reagan's insights will help you build the connection you're searching for!"—*Jake Heilbrunn, teen author of Off the Beaten Trail.*

HOW TO RAISE RESPECTFUL PARENTS
BETTER COMMUNICATION FOR TEEN AND PARENT RELATIONSHIPS

Laura Lyles Reagan

Moonshine Cove Publishing, LLC
Abbeville, South Carolina U.S.A.

ISBN: 978-1-945181-023
Library of Congress Control Number: 2016918137
Copyright 2016 by Laura Lyles Reagan

Front cover design by the author; back cover and interior design by Moonshine Cove staff.

iii

Dedication

For Hope and Grace

Acknowledgment

Thank you to the University of Texas Pan American, now the University of Texas Rio Grande Valley Sociology Department (UTRGV) where we first discussed service oriented sociology.

Thank you to UTRGV Professor Emeritus Chad Richardson, PhD, who gave me the opportunity to teach the Sociology of Childhood and Adolescence, affirming my own agency.

Thank you to Steve Harrison and his Quantum Leap team for making media-genic sense out of my hopes. Thank you to the best Quantum Leap book coach I could have, Martha Bullen.

Thank you to my dear departed friend, Frank, who read me from the start and forecast this effort by saying, "Kids need this first."

From where it all began, thank you to my childhood friend, Jim for always listening and believing.

Thank you to Gene Robinson and Moonshine Cove Publishing for taking a risk on me.

To all my family and friends who have endured my discussion about these ideas for more than a decade, thank you, patient ones -- Claudia, Michelle, Anitra, Bobby and many more.

ABOUT THE AUTHOR

Laura Lyles Reagan, known as the Teen & Parent Relationship Whisperer, is a family sociologist with more than 30 years of experience in practical youth development and parenting coaching. She holds a Masters in Sociology specializing in interactionism and communication dynamics. She is a former instructor in the Sociology of Childhood and Adolescence at the University

 of Texas Rio Grande Valley. Her original research, "Dynamic Duos" about adult mentor and parent impact on youth and teens was featured in the *Journal of Applied Social Science, 2013.*

Her teen and parent coaching service has trained parent educators at the Pharr San Juan Alamo Independent School District in the Rio Grande Valley of Texas which was funded by a grant awarded by the Raul C. Tijerina Foundation.

Laura's youth development career spans service in Mexico City as a youth substance abuse counselor to non-profit management in the Boys & Girls Club Movement. She conducts workshops on hot topics such as teen-parent communication, substance abuse, bullying prevention and teen suicide prevention in English and Spanish. She is a frequent radio guest and can be interviewed in English or Spanish. She has published over 100 articles in regional parenting magazines throughout the United States and Canada. Most importantly Laura is the mother of one teen daughter and one young adult daughter. She loves to recount their adventures. This is her first published book.

Laura's website: *www.lauralreagan.com*

Preface

Writing coaches tell their writer apprentices to write the book that they want to read. It is likely that others will want to read it too. That's what I did. I wrote the book I wanted to read when I was a teen. Time and popular culture may change but basic human need hasn't changed. The inevitable struggle between parent and emerging young adult remains.

Like many teens, I felt misunderstood by my parents. I knew they loved me but I was convinced they didn't "get me." When I went to college, I learned about the psychological perspective regarding the parent-child conflict. But it didn't help much, to label my family as dysfunctional. What did help was my study of the sociology of childhood. I learned that children and teens occupy a different social position or place in society than adults do. I also learned that children and teens can exert their own "agency" in interpreting the world and influencing their parents. Most parents will attest to this!

The reality is, parents have most of the power even if they don't think so. Parents earn the money and pay the bills while teens go to school which literally buys them more power, control and influence. Parents are still legally responsible for teens since most of the teen years are spent as minors. Parents naturally have more experience than their children which is why children and teens them as guides. Despite the power structure, teens can have a profound influence on the relationship they have with their parents. Conscious choice making and effective communication are keys.

This book can serve as a road map to building more positive relationships while honoring your own need for greater independence. The first chapter uses a popular idea of culture or sub-culture to describe the difference in roles between parents and teens. The second chapter introduces the concept of co-creation, where both parents and teens jointly define the parameters of their relationship and how it works. The subsequent companion chapters on *How to Listen So Your Parents Stop Talking* and *How to Talk So Your Parents Will Listen* describe exactly how to improve communication and negotiation skills. There are exercises to try in small or larger doses depending on your situation, along with real-life examples of teen and parent conversations. There is a chapter on difficult family situations such as substance abuse, mental illness and divorce. The final chapter applies the communication skills to the world of work and school, detailing how to use the skills outside your family. This book is a "how to" manual for navigating the adult world and empowering yourself with attitudes and communication skills that will serve you in the adult world you are joining and co-creating.

After trying some of the skills, please visit my website and share how it is working out for you at www.lauralreagan.com.

Author's Note

The approach of co-creation in teen parent communication, Parenting Sociology and Heart 2 Heart Parents does not deny mental illness and the need for treatment if mental illness is diagnosed in a parent, child or teen. The approach of Co-creation Parenting, Parenting Sociology and Heart 2 Heart Parents Parenting simply offers a set of tools for creating satisfying relationships when mental illness has been shown to not be the problem.

The terms, *adult culture* and *youth culture* are used throughout this text as a popular reference to encourage conscious agency as co-creators of the social institution of family. These terms are not being used as social science academic research terms.

Contents

How To Raise
Respectful Parents

Chapter 1 — You Are Not Alone

Do you ever feel like an alien?

Imagine you are an alien from another planet, dropped into a human family for a scientific study of this foreign species called human beings. You notice the adults make most of the decisions for the young so you will focus on them. You will need to understand their biology and be familiar with their physical needs such as food, water and sleep. You will need to develop an understanding of their social and emotional needs. You will need to try to understand the need for their institutions, like families and schools and churches.

You will need to be an anthropologist of sorts. You will have to learn their customs and rituals. You will certainly need to decipher their language and learn to speak it. Undoubtedly, you will notice the power structure of the family you landed in. You will notice that parents set the rules and make most of the decisions for the children. As a social scientist you might question if this process actually trains the young with the skills they will need for the future.

Do you ever feel as if you were an alien dropped down into a human family? Or perhaps the stork that delivers babies got the address wrong? Most of us feel that way sometime during our teen years.

Psychologists will tell you that in some ways, feeling "alien" to your family is a natural part of your development. It allows you to become independent from your family, identify with your friends and begin to make some of life's choices on your own.

You begin to choose your own value system and take what you want and don't want, from what your parents, teachers and other mentors have taught you. Your teen years allow you to change what you don't want from the models you've been given and begin to live life differently.

Some sociologists will tell you that you are kept out of society, warehoused in schools and kept from earning money, kept from having a position (job or other status) without a vote about things that affect your life. Of course you feel left out and alienated because you are! But, you are not alone. What you feel is common. It was even common for your parents during their own teen years.

You're not alone

This book will offer an approach and tools about how to interact with your parents positively even though they may feel foreign to you and you may feel "alien" to them. You can find your own voice and better express yourself using the communication skills outlined. By communicating more effectively with your parents, you will also be learning skills that will help you become a better adult communicator. These skills will help you take your place in the world as a spouse, parent, employee or employer.

The following are real examples of teens with communication issues. The teens need to communicate what is going on with them but feel inhibited in some way. These teens may not be living your exact reality but you will likely find something in common with some of them and what they feel about their relationships with their parents. Please read them with an open mind and try to identify with the similarities you share with them and don't focus on the differences.

Good Country Girl - Patti

Patti is a simple country girl. She enjoys gardening and is a member of the 4-H in her school and community. She raises rabbits for her the local livestock show. She even won second prize in her age group her sophomore year in high school. Patti has an outgoing personality and is well liked by her group friends. She lives with her mom and stepfather in the country outside of the city limits. By day, all is well — but at night when she returns home in the evening on the school bus she lives a different reality.

The thing that causes her the most pain in life is her mother's alcoholism. She gets a knot in the pit of her stomach almost every evening when she steps off the school bus. The walk down the short driveway to her front door feels like crossing a football field because of the anxiety she feels. She never knows what to expect when she walks in the door. If her mother just started drinking, she was silly and sort of fun. She could still ask questions about Patti's day. If her mom had been drinking since early in the day, there might be an argument about almost any subject. If Patti was lucky, her mom would already be passed out. Her stepdad was no help. Although he was sober as a recovering alcoholic. It seemed that staying sober took everything he had to offer.

If Patti wanted to eat, it fell to her to cook after a full eight-hour day of school and an hour bus ride. Patti was also responsible for cleaning the house and managing the farm which was enough work for a full time job. There were nights when Patti fell into bed exhausted with no energy to do her homework, wondering, how she was going to keep up with school and life.

Popular Kid — Myra

Myra is one of those drop dead gorgeous girls. Her teeth are perfect. Her smile lights up a room. Her deep brown eyes dance when she laughs. Even her figure is perfect. She never has a bad hair day and yes, to add to the cliché she is a cheerleader. She knows how to navigate the political power structure in high school and doesn't seem to make waves. She's the person you want to have as your best friend because she is loyal to a fault. To her credit, she is generally kind to others. She can have any boy in the school and knows it. So, she gets the smart ones to do her homework for her.

She never cracks a book but always makes good grades because she is popular. The teachers call on her but excuse her when she doesn't know the answer. Because she skates along using her good looks to get what she wants and doesn't work hard to merit any real accomplishment, she is secretly, terribly insecure. She thinks no one will like her for who she truly is. Her parents always told her she was beautiful but she wonders why they don't have big dreams for her.

Misfit Jock - Jeff

Jeff is a big lineman on his high school football team. He is a huggable gentle giant with blond hair and green eyes. He does well in school and sings in the choir. He will likely follow in his grandfather's footsteps and join the military because his eyes light up when he talks about the service. He is almost too kind and too good. The girls take advantage of him. He wants to be in the popular crowd but never quite fits in. He seems to have trouble finding that special girl and he wears out his friends talking about the fictitious character.

No one understands why he lacks confidence because they like him. Maybe Jeff is embarrassed about his working-class family and dorky sisters. He doesn't have the clothes or the car that his rich friends have. He dreams of getting out of his hometown one day and making something of himself. He is tired of feeling used by everyone — even by his mom and dad. He wishes he could tell them how he really feels.

Punk Kid — Kim

Kim is a punk rocker in a town with "0" punk rockers. She identifies with the "be your own person," rage against the system lyrics. She is tall, think, beautiful and has soulful deep blue eyes. She has punk cut, blue hair and feels most at home in a mosh pit. Even though her hair and look scream, "pay attention," she is quite shy. She has an anxiety disorder but rejects medication. She believes she can control it by venting through her music. Music is also an escape from her stepparents. Yes, stepparents. She can't imagine her parents ever married to each other, but she doesn't understand why each parent had to pick such losers for partners and give her such wacky stepparents. She is sick of hearing about her clothes from her stepmother and her loud music from her stepfather. What do they know anyway?

She mainly tries to avoid her stepparents and only interact with each parent. She loves them but she wishes she could communicate what she was really feeling. Kim writes poetry. Some of it is dark. Sometimes she leaves her poetry book out on her bed so her mom will find it and read it. She wishes she could share all of who she is with her parents.

She wishes they would give her as much attention as they give their partners.

The Criminal — Sam

Sam grew up poor. He is the middle child of five. He learned early that negative attention was better than no attention. As a boy, he had cute, curly hair but he was embarrassed by it. He was embarrassed and self-conscious about almost everything. But he loved to learn and was always in the library reading. His special interest was mythology. Because he read a lot, he almost always knew the answer when the teacher would ask questions in class discussion. But he was too embarrassed or self-conscious to raise his hand. When he was called on, he purposely answered wrong. He was too cool to play the role of the nerd or smart kid. His intelligence did cause others to look up to him.

He is a charismatic leader and has a great sense of humor. People follow him.

Unfortunately, he was often in trouble at school for being the cut up or for setting others up to take the brunt of the joke. He is a petty thief too but he never gets caught because he anticipates almost every angle and consequence. These skills could have been used on the chessboard but he never wanted that kind of positive attention.

His mother is mentally ill. She beat him as a boy and even as a teen. It causes Sam great shame. He vowed to never strike his mother when she has one of her episodes. Sam feels torn between taking care of his mother and wanting to run away. Sam's sister is an adult and lives with her own family. Sam's mom and dad divorced when Sam was a boy. It falls to Sam to figure out what to do about his mother. Even as a boy he sensed she wasn't herself. Sam long forgot how to talk about his feelings with anyone because he trusts no one.

The Artist — Joe

Joe is a naturally gifted artist. Like most artists he is moody and quiet. He was a happy little boy but his family doesn't "get" him. His dad wants him to go hunting and fishing with him. He bought Joe a gun for his twelfth birthday. Joe had no idea what to do with it. He went on a deer hunt with his dad but refused to shoot anything. Joe took his sketch pad instead but his dad didn't complement his creativity. He scolded Joe about things like not holding the gun right. His dad certainly didn't take an interest in his drawings. In high school when Joe had an opportunity for a summer internship in a college, his mom thought his summer might be better used to earn money with a summer job.

Joe's parents love him but they just don't understand why he can't be more practical. They don't understand why he can't be more like them. Joe is an introvert anyway but his parents' lack of understanding and appreciation of his gifts make him feel alone. His parents don't have money saved up for his college. Joe has dreams of going to art school or a major university. He wishes he had the words to tell his parents about his dreams.

What do each of these teens want and need?

Each teen wants to be their own person while maintaining a positive connection with their families. Some even want to make a positive difference in the world using their gifts and talents.

Youth development specialists from the Boys & Girls Club of America as well as other youth serving organizations and professionals such as psychologists and sociologists have determined that healthy youth development includes the following components.

- A sense of belonging

The first place we "fit" and are accepted is with our families. In our teen years, we can gain a sense of belonging from our peer group, school or church group.

- A sense of power and influence

All children need to be heard with the opportunity to influence the decisions and actions of others. This begins in the family and then extends to other groups.

- A sense of usefulness

- This is the feeling that youth have of contributing to others, providing a valued service or occupying an important role.

-   **A sense of competence**

All youth need to explore their gifts and talents and feel that there is something they can do well.

We achieve these important developments by effectively communicating who we are.

Teens face numerous crises given the overwhelming high school dropout rates, child and adolescent obesity rates, substance abuse, bullying, teenage pregnancy rates and juvenile crime rates rising. A multitude of studies show that teens still view their parents as their primary role models.

The following chapters and exercises will help you improve your relationship with your parents. You will learn how to listen so they don't lecture you and you will learn to talk in a way that will make them take notice. As a result, your relationship will be less conflictual and you may even learn to enjoy your parents more! These same communication skills will help you with your friends, your teachers and eventually your employers as you grow and change.

The purpose of parenting is to help kids and teens gain the skills and resources they need to be successful adults. The purpose of your teen years is to grow your skills over time to become a successful adult as you define success. Parents and teens have complementary, not competing roles in the endeavor to grow, even though sometimes all you feel is conflict.

By empowering yourself as a growing teen with effective communication skills, you can fully participate in creating a complementary, satisfying relationship with your parents that fulfills its purpose of preparing you for the future!

This book will help you build the skills and the relationship you need.

Chapter 2 - From *They* to *We*:

Co-creating a Positive Relationship with Your Parents

Let's go back to the idea of being an alien anthropologist from another planet sent to study, understand, negotiate and begin peaceful productive relations with the new sub-culture of human beings called adults. What are the tools you would need to operate in their world?

As ridiculous as it seems, it may serve you to think about relating to your parents as if you don't know them. Let's face it! The adult world and by default your parents, can be confusing, overwhelming, illogical and chaotic. Social science tools might help create some order from the chaos.

Here are a few of the tools you might need to investigate your new surroundings and learn the culture of adults and their language.

- **Non-judgmental Attitude**

This is their culture. In order to learn it, we must assume that they do things the way they do for a reason. We might not agree or like that reason but it is uniquely theirs. If we try to understand it and not judge it, we may learn how to relate to adults better.

Viewing your parents non-judgementally will actually serve to empower you to consider how you chose to relate to them rather than feeling victim to the way things have always been.

If your parents have a 10:00 p.m. bedtime, rather than seeing them as lame for going to bed early, consider that they work in a job they may hate in order to pay the bills.

If your parents cook at home most of the time, rather than go out to eat, consider not only the expense but also the fact that they may want to eat healthier and can accomplish their weight loss goals more easily by eating at home.

- **Be Curious — Be a Student of Adult Culture**

Ask why things work the way they do?

Dad, why do you think it's important to have a curfew? (At this point, don't argue with the answer, just grow in your understanding of why parents believe what they believe.)

Mom, why do you think college is important?
Sometimes, I really want to be able to make weekend plans. I know family time is important but why is it so important to you that Sunday dinners can't be missed?

- **Use the scientific method for your social learning and social experiment. Form a hypothesis. Gather evidence.**

Every parent wants their child to do better than they have. If your parents are insistent on sending you to college, ask how many other family members have gone to college. Perhaps no one has and you will be the first. They may be investing their hopes of a college future on you in terms of improving the family. They may not have been able to put it into words as to why it is so important to them that you go to college.

- **Validate your Hypothesis or Findings by using multiple sources**

Ask your friends about their parents. Do they have similar rules as your parents? Do they use their weekends the same way your parents do?

Parent Culture

Parents want their children to have a better life than they did. They want you to be happier, be able to take care of yourself, have a better job than they have, have a better marriage than they have (no offense to mom and dad) and they want you to be a better parent than they are. Honestly, it's true! Even the worst parent in the penitentiary wants their child to have a better life of freedom than they do.

The trouble is, sometimes parents don't recognize that you are your own person now. Once they did everything for you. Once upon a time, you were completely dependent upon them. Now, you have your own likes and dislikes. You have your own desires about the future. You no longer need them in the same ways you did. Sometimes, it's hard for parents to relinquish responsibility of you and the control that goes with it, even if they know that they should.

Lessons Learned from Being a Social Scientist of Parental Adult Culture

1. Adults respect order.

The clearer you can be in how you present yourself and your ideas, the more readily adults were hear, understand and respect you.

Hint: Plan your talk about sensitive subjects. Write down an outline and stick to the script you prepare.

2. Adults like kids who sound like them.

We tend to have a bias towards people like us. We like others who look and sound like we do. Without diversity training, bosses tend to hire employees who are similar to them. As human beings, parents are the same way.

Hint: Listen to the language your parents use. Pay attention to their vocabulary. When you want to communicate about an emotionally charged subject, copy their phrases.

3. Adults need reassurance.

It is a biological instinct for parents to protect their young. It is literally hard wired into their DNA. As a result, parents have fear about their children's safety and well-being. The more a teen can be sensitive to and prepare for this legitimate biological and psychological need the better communication will be.

Hint: Parents will be impressed if you tell them before you ask how you intend to pay for an item or who will chaperone the party you want to attend or that you know to locate the police officers at a concert when you walk in. They will be comforted by the fact that you have thought ahead for emergency situations and are taking safety into account.

Learning about parent culture and translating your ideas to adult-speak will help you practice communication skills that will help you be successful in college, find employment and develop professionally.

Teen Culture

Social scientists have observed that children create meaning from the world around them and work together to create their own interpretations of even complicated issues like racism and gender roles. But adults often miss out on kid culture and its creative force because they are too busy imparting adult culture. Or adults are too busy with their own lives. Ever heard of the **generation gap?**

Since cars were invented and teens asked for the keys on weekends and had a separate time away from parents, **teens have been creating their own culture.** Rock and roll was born as a result! Today teens create their own language, meanings and of course music. Teen culture and various subcultures are dynamic and ever changing. It flies at the speed of the internet through social media.

In other parts of the world, the generations are not so divided. While the amount of time spent with each other daily is greater in tribal cultures when compared to our own Western culture, are we doomed to be disengaged as parents and teens?

No! We have choices. One powerful choice is to co-create the relationship you want with your parents.

Co-creation 101

Co-creating is a sociological and even a business term about relationships. It suggests that each party in a relationship shares the ability or power to influence the relationship. Traditional sociology views the role of children and teens as passive recipients of social learning where the institutions of society such as family, school and church teach children about our culture's beliefs and behaviors.

As any new parent knows, children can definitely define the relationship by expressing their needs. Babies cry. Parents feed them, pick them up or change diapers. That influence continues throughout the child's life as they learn and grow to full maturity.

In the new sociology of childhood, children are co-creators of culture and relationships. Their role is obviously different than that of adults but their influence as what sociologists call "social actors" is powerful. (Prout & James 2010).

What if teens claimed their rightful power as co-creators and consciously chose to influence their relationship with their parents? What if through simple, honest communication and a little education and experimentation, teens could positively influence their parents and by so doing, practice the skills they will need for adulthood?

Co-Creation: You Can Help Create a Better Relationship with Your Parents

Co-creation is a conscious effort between teens and parents to be fully involved in jointly defining the relationship.

Unconscious Co-creation

Co-creation happens all the time unconsciously. We teach people how to treat us based on our own behavior. When your dad comes in tired and stressed from a full day at work, you probably know it's not a good time to ask for money.

Co-creation also occurs when your mom or dad decides it's not worth the battle to remind you for the third time to take out the trash and they do it themselves.

Or they read your response in your eyes about the choice of family vacation when you were planning something else so they get mad at you before you before you even say anything.

To use the power of co-creation consciously simply means to build a more positive relationship with your parents by the way you choose to communicate with them. If you take a pro-active role with them, they may begin to see you as the growing, developing mature young adult you are becoming.

a.) Their Job

A parent's job in the teen years is to prepare their teen for the future. This is an impossible task because they have no idea what the future will look like. They don't know what the economy will be like. Will we all be looking for oil? Or will there be water wars? Will teens need to have survival skills as the doomsday movies predict? Parents don't know what the culture will be like.

How will global warming affect our fashion, lifestyle and career choices? Will everyone keep a garden at home? Will art be viewed in person or will we have access to it online? Will we all speak English or is it necessary for teens to know Spanish, since Latinos are the fast growing segment of the U.S. population? No parent can predict the future.

Myths

i. **Parents know everything.**

They don't.

ii. My parents don't love me, care about me or get me.

Yes, they do. Its healthy self-interest for them to love you. All parents have a biological if not spiritual imperative to see they children better off than they are. Parents don't always have the tools to show you how much they love you.

iii. My parents are the worst.

They aren't. You can always find someone with worse parents than you have.

b.) Your Job

A teen's job is to grow to be a healthy adult physically, mentally, emotionally and spiritually, learning enough about the world to become self-sufficient in time. To do this requires increasing independence from parents while identifying with friends (usually other teens close to your age) and mentors (teachers, older siblings and young adults that are already making it on their own). Choosing the right friends, mentors and resources is critical to help you develop into the kind of adult you want to be.

Growing away from parents and towards your adult self requires building positive trusting relationships with others. These friends and mentors become the bridge to your adult self. It's a paradox.

By becoming independent from your parents you become more reliant on others who will help you become an adult. Your job as a teen is about finding the people and resources you need to become a healthy responsible adult.

Myths

i. **Everyone thinks they know where they are going and how to get**

They don't! They are just as scared, insecure and nervous as you feel.

ii. **Everyone thinks they know what's best for you**.

They don't! There has never been a "you" in the history of the universe. You are wonderfully unique. Even if you are a twin, despite shared DNA, how you process the world is still unique.

iii. **No one has ever had it as bad as I do or feels as bad I do.** *

As unique as you are, what you feel isn't. It's a paradox. What about Anne Frank, spending her adolescence in a closet by day and a small room by night in a war-torn country only to be captured and killed in the end? What about teens growing up with famine in Africa lucky enough to make it to a refugee camp? You may feel bad, but feelings are not facts when compared to reality in most of our cases.

*Nevertheless, there are some things that are unacceptable. Physical, verbal or sexual abuse is never okay. Abuse of any kind is too much for any teen or family to deal with alone. Get professional help. See Chapter 7 for some resources for how to seek help.

An Example of Co-creation

My youngest daughter loves horses. She has been riding since she was four years old. In her mid-teens, she discovered an approach of interacting with horses popularized by Monty Roberts, who is considered one of the first horse whisperers. He was made famous by the book, *Shy Boy* which is the story of a wild mustang that communicated with Monty and followed him home. Mr. Roberts attributes this to the language of *equis.* It is the non-verbal communication horses use to communicate with each other.

By observing the non-verbal communication of horses, Mr. Roberts learned it over time and applied it to communicate with horses in their "language." By learning horses' language and behaviors, a human can interact with a horse in a way that invites partnership instead of submission to control and domination. Parent and teen cultural communication is like that! When parents and teens understand the motivations of each and communicate in a way that is understood by both, positive things can happen.

By tuning into one another, meeting the horse with its own language (non-verbal communication and behaviors) a human can literally co-create a relationship with another species. Ask any teen or tween if their parents are alien to them and at some point during their adolescence they will likely agree. Because of focusing on the non-verbal part of communication, we can learn something about the importance of actively, co-creating a relationship from the example of the horse whisperer that can be applied to the parent-teen relationship.

Relationship Building

Teens and specialists through research have identified ways to tune into each other and influence each other's lives from the perspective of parent and teen.

I served as Executive Director of a youth development non-profit for seven years. We ran mentoring programs and youth development curriculum with specific targeted outcomes. We wanted to help our youth members grow to be healthy and successful, meaning we helped them graduate high school, develop without substance abuse, avoid childhood obesity and prevent teenage pregnancy.

We achieved these results by providing a meaningful relationship with a caring adult. When we evaluated these programs we saw trends in what kids perceived as the important factors for how adults impact them. Invariably, the first adults they spoke of were their parents. This was even true for our teen focus group and survey results.

Teens admire their parents for 1) doing fun activities with them, 2) teaching them a skill, 3) protecting them, 4) help them solve problems and 5) are present in times of crisis.

The following descriptions and sample responses are the ways teens identified as important for how they were influenced by parents and mentors.

Fun activities — include but not limited to: games, sports, movies and shared events including family outings.

Mom took me shopping last weekend!

Dad played video games with me almost every night this summer.

Every Tuesday is family board game night. At first I thought it was lame but when my parents let us eat junk food while we do it, it's not so bad. It's sort a cool!" My dad won't let me win though. He so competitive. Mom always lets us win.

My mom and I go to the dollar movies and watch the romantic comedies since dad hates them. She laughs really loud. It's embarrassing but also cool to see her let her hair down.

Teaching skills refers to homework help, coaching of a sport, guitar lessons, dance lessons, computer skills and much more.

Mom taught me to Zumba. I taught her cooler dance steps.

Dad was the first one to teach me football. We used to play in the backyard.

Dad is a math whiz. He helps me with algebra. I still don't get it but at least he tries to help.

My grandmother taught me to sew one summer. I thought it would be boring but now I really like it. It's relaxing.

Caretaking and protection refers to protection from bullying and providing for needs such as meals, clothes and healthcare when ill.

My parents buy me new school clothes and supplies every year. It makes me feel good.

My mom has two jobs. But every weekend, we get a pizza or something like that. When we get back she cooks most of the afternoon. She freezes the meals for us and we heat them up when we get home from school. She works really hard for us. She wants me to study hard and get one good job that pays enough for everything. I want to get a job that pays me a lot so she can retire. My mom really loves us.

Every day I walked home from school. There was a group of guys that used to bully me. One day I got up the courage to tell my dad. He told me to walk home another way. I did but the bullies followed me. My dad drove up right behind them and honked. They ran away but my dad caught one and told them if they didn't stop he was going to report them. I didn't have any trouble after that. I think my dad saved my life!

Problem solving responses included but are not limited to hard homework, help with bullying, trouble with a boyfriend /girlfriend or teacher, a parent's divorce or substance abuse.

My dad looked everywhere when my puppy ran away. We drove around, calling and calling her. We looked for hours. He thought he heard her barking. He walked through muddy ditches until he finally found her. She was all wet and smelled terrible. I wrapped her in a towel and dried her off. She was crying so much that I started crying. I think my dad cried too. My dad showed me he really cared.

I don't understand algebra. I don't understand why we have to take it. We won't use it later in life. My mom said she had trouble in math in high school also. She knew I was studying but I wasn't getting it. She couldn't help me. But she hired a tutor even though she really couldn't afford it. It made a big difference.

Sara's boyfriend grabbed her arm and twisted it when he thought she was talking to another guy and stepping out on him. I told Sara that wasn't right and she shouldn't take abusive behavior from anyone. I was really worried about Sara but I didn't want to be a snitch. When Sara came over to my house, my mom saw the mark and asked about it. Sara said it was an accident but Mom asked me about it later. I was glad she saw because she is going to talk to Sara's parents or the counselor or something.

Presence in crisis examples include but are not limited to: loss of a pet, feelings of social isolation, school failure, boyfriend/girlfriend break ups, family distress over economics, alcoholism, drug abuse or divorce.

When my dad called my teacher about re-testing after I failed. I felt like he really cared.

When my grandmother died, my mom was really upset. My stepfather helped her out and helped her make decisions. It was like he took over. I felt left out but my dad came to the funeral and sat by me even though he and my stepfather don't really get along.

Chris broke up with me over the weekend. I cried and cried all day Saturday. By Sunday, my mom said, it was time to deal with it and move on. At first I thought she was being mean, then she showed me the ice cream and DVDs she bought. We spent the whole day on the couch together, eating junk food and watching old movies. Even though we didn't really talk about Chris much, I knew she understood. I felt a little better by the time I went back to school on Monday."

My research was featured in the *Journal of Applied Social Science* (JASS, 2013) and shows what these teens believe to be impactful for them about how parents and other caring adults can influence them. These areas of fun activities, teaching a skill, protection and caretaking, problem solving and presence in crisis, can be used to build more positive relationships with your parents.

Take a few minutes to think about whether or not you identify with these teens. Do you feel more connected to your parents if you do fun activities together? Are you more willing to listen to them if they help you with a problem? Do you feel closer to them if they are there for you in a crisis moment? Take a few moments to consider the things you can do to build a more positive relationship with your parents by "tuning into them" as people. Exercise A may help you.

Exercise A — Relationship Building

Fill out this simple questionnaire and follow the suggestions to co-create a better relationship with your parents, starting today.

1.) What fun activities can you share? Name at least three. Then ask your parent(s) to do one of these things this weekend with you. Don't ask for anything else when you are asking them to make time for fun with you.

a.) _____

b.) _____

c.) _____

2.) Think of three skills your parent(s) taught you. Write them down no matter how small they seem. Then thank your parent for teaching you that. (Yes, it may seem corny or hokey but trust me, it will make your parents day and help build a more positive relationship.)

a.) _____
b.) _____
c.) _____

3.)   Think of three things your parent(s) has done to protect you or take care of you. Write them below and then look for an opportunity. You may even consider writing a thank you note or putting a personal hand written note inside a holiday card like Christmas, Mother's Day, Father's Day or their birthday.

a.) _____
b.) _____
c.) _____

4.) Write down three problems your parent(s) helped you solve. The next meal you have together, tell them the following. *I was thinking about the time you helped me solve that problem (name the problem). Thanks for helping me with that.*

a.) _____
b.) _____
c.) _____

5.) Were your parents ever there for you when you were in crisis? Name the crisis

and try to be there for them the next time you see them super stressed.

a.) _____
b.) _____
c.) _____

Co-creation Means Re-Negotiation

When teens and parents re-negotiate the power structure of their relationship in a way that honors the importance of both of their roles and share responsibility for a positive relationship, they both feel better, enjoy each other and prepare for the future. Relating to each other becomes less about one correcting the other or one blaming the other and more about uniting together to solve problems. The "you" and "me" becomes "we."

A parent has to balance two responsibilities, 1) keep you safe so you can grow up healthy and 2) give you the resources and support you need to explore and find your place in the world so that you become a caring, responsible, contributing member of society. Balancing those two objectives is a monumental task and NO ONE gets it right all the time.

As a teen, you MUST 1) push against the boundaries that parents and other authority figures set for your safety so that YOU can discover for yourself what is safe for you. And 2) you MUST explore the world, find your own resources (some of which your parents have given you) and make them your own for your life's journey.

Your parents' roles and responsibilities and your roles and responsibilities may seem to be directly against each other but they exist for a reason. They need to be different. The different roles and responsibilities of parents to teens, actually provide you with the testing ground to experiment with who you want to become. That means the conflicts you have with your parents and other adults actually help you define who you are. Over time, you get to choose what you want to keep about what they have taught you and what you want to discard. The perceived conflicts, help you set the stage to be able to advocate and negotiate for your needs and wants. Communicating and advocating for your needs and wants are skills you will need as an adult in all your personal and professional relationships.

Rather than resenting your parents for doing their job, why not see their position as the very thing that can help you grow to adulthood. The co-creation attitudes and communication skills can help you do the work of growing into the adult you want, by practicing with your parents. The co-creation approach begins by defining who in the relationship has specific issues and builds to learn ways to listen and speak so your parents will stop their talking and hear you

Chapter 3 - Shades of Gray: Whose Problem Is It?

I am a parenting coach. Often parents come to my coaching sessions seeking a "solution" for how to control their children. I point out that it is their teen's job to test the boundaries, experiment, explore their world. It is their teen's job to try to understand the world and interpret meaning from it and grow. Controlling behavior often works against the natural desire everyone has to learn and grow.

The process of co-creating the relationship means that parents and teens can relate in a way that meets the drives of both roles, parent and teen. The parent can fulfill his role as protector and guide, while the teen can fulfill her role as a growing independent human being.

To help teens and parents become "we" requires these four key components, defining, hearing, speaking and practicing. These are the session topics of co-creation that I use at Heart 2 Heart Parents during the parenting coaching sessions I facilitate. These components can be initiated by either parents or teens. The following chapters will explain these in detail with different teen scenarios to help illustrate the ideas about communication.

First you will review how to define the problem with an exercise called, "Whose problem is it?" in Chapter 3. Then you will learn to hear your parent's perspective, in Chapter 4, entitled, "How to Listen so your Parents Stop Talking." In Chapter 5, "Speak so Your Parents Hear You," you will learn to speak and be heard with your perspective respected. In Chapter 6, you will put it all together by reviewing and practicing the communication skills. This chapter will give you ways to sustain the co-creation model.

Problem Definition — Whose problem is it?

Parents and teens are often confused about whether or not an issue is the teen's problem to solve or the parent's problem to solve. Sometimes, it's a mutual problem that both have to work on. Respecting who has the responsibility to deal with a situation is really helpful to establish the positive communication you want with each other.

Your teen years are your opportunity to make mistakes and learn from them, while still under the protection of your parents. This means your parents need to be willing to let you make mistakes. You can educate them about the concept of natural consequences.

Natural consequences occur when the next logic action or result is allowed to take place without any interference from an outside force (such as parents).

Sometimes it's easier to see the concept illustrated with examples from kids rather than teens.

a.) Tom

Tom forgot his lunchbox. He has some options. He can skip lunch. Or he can ask for help and borrow lunch money from the cafeteria lady or a friend and eat lunch in the cafeteria. Hopefully, this negative result will help Tom remember his lunch box packed with his favorite things tomorrow.

b.) Clara

Clara's spelling test is on Friday. Clara is not a good speller and really has to study hard in order to make good grades in spelling. But Clara's favorite TV show is on Thursday nights and she really wants to stay up late and watch it. She does and suffers the consequences. She makes a bad grade on her spelling test. Clara has some choices. She can take this as a learning opportunity and study ahead of time on Tuesday and Wednesday nights so that all she needs is a quick review on Thursdays or she can skip her Thursday night show. With either choice Clara is learning to make better decisions about her priorities and manage her time better.

Parents care about their kids and want them to do well. Tom's parents want him to eat healthy, nutritious meals and Clara's parents want her to do well in school. By allowing each child to deal with the natural consequences or natural results of their behavior, the kids are learning to solve problems themselves responsibly.

Teen examples are similar but may be a little more complicated. Review these scenarios, write down your answer, then review the discussion afterwards to see how your thoughts compare. Remember there are no right or wrong answers. There are only perspectives from the different roles of parent and teen. Discussing these issues might shed some light on the work you need to do to reach some common ground about your independent roles.

Exercise B - Whose problem is it?

1.) Tim wants to borrow the family car this weekend to take his girlfriend to the game and pizza afterwards. Tim has a valid driver's license and is on his parents' insurance. His parents pay for these things because Tim has agreed to pick his sister up from her afternoon program; therefore, Tim contributes to the family welfare by helping with his sister since his parents both work late and can't pick up the sister. He is rewarded by being placed on the family insurance. Tim doesn't have enough money for gas and the game and pizza. He doesn't get paid from his part time job till next week. Whose problem is it to find or earn money for his date?

2.) Mom wants help with the housework. It's Saturday, Jon's only day to sleep late since he goes to school and works. He told his mom he would vacuum and mop over the weekend but he didn't say exactly when. Mom wants to wake up Jon at 8:30am to do the floors. Whose problem is it?

3.) Sara is failing algebra. She has been going to tutoring but she just isn't getting it. Sara wants to drop the class and change her schedule and try again next semester because she will have a lighter class load. She needs her parents' permission to do so. Whose problem is it?

4.) Jim told Dad he would mow the lawn when he got back from football practice on Saturday. He finished Saturday morning practice but then went out to lunch with his teammates. He came home mid-afternoon and dad was mowing the lawn. He changed his clothes and went outside to take over for his dad but dad didn't let him have the mower. He could tell dad was angry. Whose problem is it?

5.) Jessica's boyfriend is verbally abusive with her. She hasn't told anyone except her best friend Michelle. Michelle thinks she should break up with him, but Jessica loves him. Jessica says he promises he won't do it again. Michelle told Jessica she is afraid for her and will tell an adult if it happens again. Jessica says her parents wouldn't do anything anyway. Whose problem is it?

6.) Patti's mom is passed out on the couch again when Patti gets home from school. Mom has been drinking all afternoon. Patti needs to have a permission slip signed by tomorrow for a band trip. Patti makes her own dinner and something for her mom who doesn't wake up to eat it. Patti decides to forge her signature and puts the paper in her backpack. Is there a problem?

7.) Myra has a date Friday as usual. Her parents have an old-fashioned rule about meeting her dates. She tells her mom that it's a group thing so she doesn't have to introduce him. Mom suspects Myra is lying because the place they were going has changed a few times. Mom called the mother of Myra's best friend Maria. Mom doesn't get any details about the evening because Maria isn't going on this particular outing. Mom decides to trust her daughter and not confront Myra. Whose problem is it?

8.) Jeff wants to go to college but his parents barely make enough money to pay the bills. There are other children in the family to consider too. Jim's parents don't have a college fund for any of the children. Jeff started the application process and has even filled out a few scholarship applications for state schools. But he decides not to apply for the college he really wants to go to because it's an out of state, private university. He believes it will be too tough financially. Whose problem is it?

9.) Sam was picked up for loitering outside a pool hall over the weekend. Even if his mom wanted to bail him out, she couldn't afford it since she is a single mom trying to work three part-time jobs to make ends meet. Sam didn't show up for school Monday morning because he was still in jail. Sam's girlfriend picked up some of his homework so he wouldn't get further behind. Both the women in his life wanted him to do better and at least graduate high school. Sam is stuck with a public defender and would have to wait for arraignment. Whose problem is it?

10.) Joe needs new and expensive professional charcoal and colored pencils for his drawings. His parents see the pencils as a luxury and want Joe to pay for them. Joe doesn't have a job to earn money for them yet. Whose problem is it?

Scenario Discussions:

1.) Tim — Gas & Pizza Money

Tim's date and the money to fund his activities are his responsibility. We aren't told directly but it seems like that is the agreement in place between Tim and his parents. Since Tim won't get paid before date night, he must either cancel the date which he presumably doesn't not want to do or ask for a loan from his parents. If he shares from the heart how important this date is to him (using I-Messages as discussed in Chapter 5) he may be able to secure the loan. If his parents feel he should have planned his finances better and not used up last week's paycheck, he may have problems. Generally, it seems this is Tim's problem. Do you agree? Why or why not?

2.) Jon — Housework Help

Jon is more than willing to help with the housework. He knows how hard his mom works as a single parent and he believes he should help out. Saturday is his only day to sleep in. Jon will gladly do the floors in the afternoon before he goes out that evening but he forgot to have that conversation with his mom before he went to bed Friday night. Jon's mom is waking him up Saturday morning because she wants to enjoy a fully clean house most of the weekend and get the chores behind her.

This is a problem for both mother and son because they haven't communicated clearly about it. Each perspective has validity. As a parenting coach, I would ask the mom to let go of her expectations on timing and consider it a gift that her son is willing to do the floors without a fight. I would encourage Jon to negotiate the specifics about the timing of the chore prior to Saturday so his sleep isn't interrupted. I believe this is Mom's problem. She should let go. Do you agree? Why or why not?

3.)   Sara — Algebra

Sara has tried everything this semester to learn algebra, extra homework, tutoring sessions with the teacher and private tutoring sessions. She is just one of those students who will have to take the course a second time in order for the concepts to sink in. She wants to preserve her Grade Point Average and drop the class. She has already worked it out with the teacher and administration. She just needs her parents' permission. Sara has already solved the problem and demonstrated responsibility. This was

Sara's problem to solve and she did. Do you agree? Why or why not?

4.) Jim — Mowing

This is an interesting situation. Everyone has a part in this communication problem. Like Jon's situation in scenario #2, Jim didn't have a problem mowing. He saw it as a continuation of his Saturday workout but he did not think there was a deadline on the chore. Dad didn't think he had to communicate about timing because he didn't give permission for Jim to stay out with his friends. He thought he would come home right after practice. Both should communicate more clearly. If Jim didn't have permission to go out to lunch, he should apologize and deal with the consequences. Since dad wasn't clear about when he wanted the yard mowed, dad should let that part go and pass the lawnmower to Jim. Do you agree they both have a communication problem? Why or why not?

5.) Jessica, Boyfriend and Michelle

Jessica has a big problem but she doesn't see it. Michelle has a problem because she is confronted with a very adult situation, how to deal with the issue of abuse. Michelle needs to recognize this is bigger than her teen abilities right now and confide in an adult. It can be her parents, teacher, counselor or other responsible, caring mentor. They all have problems. Do you agree? Why or why not?

6.) Patti and Permission Slip

The problem is alcoholism and Patti's mom needs help. Please see Chapter 6 for more information. In this particular situation, Patti should leave a note for her mom when she wakes up and inform her that she had to sign the permission slip on her behalf in case of an emergency, Patti's mom needs to know what is happening. Like the scenario above, Patti needs to reach out to another parent figure (possibly a stepparent) or a caring, adult mentor and let them know what she is dealing with, on a daily basis. Do you agree? Why or why not?

7.) Myra, Mom and Maria

Let's face it. Myra lied and got caught. She has a problem for sure! Lying is symptomatic of deeper issues which are treated in similar scenarios in Chapter 4 and 5. Myra and her mom need to work on their relationship to build trustworthiness, trust and better communication. Do you agree? Why or why not?

8.) Jeff and College Apps

Jeff has made the college application process, his problem and his problem alone. His parents may not have money but they care about him and may be able to help with suggestions about scholarship opportunities. Or they may be willing to go to the counselor's office at school and search the database for scholarships for him. Jim has the biggest problem because he is trying to carry his future on his own shoulders all by himself. Jim needs to communicate with his parents. Do you agree? Why or why not?

9.) Sam and Public Defender

This is solely Sam's problem. Mom needs to let the natural and logical consequences of Sam's actions run their course. Do you agree? Why or why not?

10.) Joe and Pencils

This one is easy. Get a job, Joe! If you can keep up with school and work, get a job to support your "habit," talent and obsession — drawing and painting. Do you agree? Why or why not?

Using the communication skills of active listening and I-Messages in the following chapters, you will be able to effectively communicate with your parents, exactly who has the problem in your opinion and who needs to deal with the solution for it. Your parents may not be used to your new assertive role but they will grow to respect it if you follow it up with positive action — such taking care of the problem.

Chapter 4 - How to Listen So Your Parents Stop Talking

Let's face it. Most parents talk too much. We (because I am a parent too) seem to feel this pressure to impart all that they have learned about the world to you. Sometimes they try to do it in one sitting. Learning communication skills can cut down on the opportunities for lecturing because you will be taking a more pro-active role in the relationship.

If you want your parents to trust you and stop lecturing, there are times when you will need to listen to them. If you want your parents to hear your perspective then in all fairness, you have to be willing to hear their perspective. It takes an investment of time and energy but it will pay off in the long run, because they won't feel as great a need to try to persuade you about their point of view.

Three skills can help build better relationships with your parents. Using them over time, can help you communicate more positively and effectively. The first skill is active listening and will be covered in this capture. Each teen — parent relationship conversation will be carried over to the next chapter to demonstrate the second and third skills which are open ended questions and I-Messages.

Used together and practiced often, these three skills can help you develop a direct style of communication which will help you relate to your parents better and more effectively, negotiating more of what you want and help both your parents and you have a more satisfying, less conflictual relationship.

There are two types of listening, passive listening and active listening.

Passive listening involves silence on the listener's part with attention on what is being said but no active role on the listener's part, except for hearing and hearing alone.

Active listening involves the listener in an active role with the speaker. The listener acts as a conversational mirror by reflecting the message of what is being shared.

Components of Active Listening

Active listening involves reflecting back the feeling of what your parent is saying to you. Parents feel valued when teens actively listen to them. Active listening restates the last word or phrase that your parent communicates.

- **Re-state or reflect the last phrase in as few words as possible**. When there is a natural pause in the conversation, simply repeat the last few words of the last sentence of the speaker. It may feel mechanical at first but it shows your parent that you are really listening to them and are trying to understand their meaning. Active listening also sends the message that you are interested in learning more.

- **Confirm your parent's meaning. Don't assume your understanding.** Check it out by putting a question mark with your intonation at the end of what you re-stated or by simply asking, do I understand you correctly? This step requires a little bravery because you risk rejection if you don't get their meaning the first time.

Summarize — When the conversation starts winding down, summarize the essence of the conversation to confirm meaning and build trust. It may feel awkward at first but with practice can make your parents stop feeling as if they need to lecture you.

The following conversations use active listening skills and other communication skills, primarily Open Ended Questions and I-Messages. The former ones will be explained in the next chapter about talking to your parents. For now, just observe how the conversations flow without getting bogged down in the labels.

Here is an example of a conversation with one of our teens that puts the steps together. Patti, our Country Girl actively listens to her stepfather.

Patti's Gate

Stepdad: Patti, if I told you once I told you a thousand times, close the gate back after you feed the goats.

(Patti knows she closed the gate. She always closes the gate but one of those pesky goats has learned to open it and now she is getting blamed for it. To keep from screaming at her stepfather, she decided to use active listening. By reflecting back his meaning to him she gave herself the space she needed to gain control of her feelings of being upset about being blamed.)

Patti: You want me to double check the gate to make sure it's closed. **Active Listening Reflection**

Stepdad: Yes. I always tell you that. So, did you? **Confirmation of Meaning with a question follow up**

Patti: Yes, I did close it. I did double check. I think a goat has learned how to open it.

Stepdad: Oh, okay. Maybe it's time for a different gate.

Patti: You think it's time for a different gate? I agree. **Active Listening, reflection and agreement**

Stepdad: I'll get a new latch tomorrow.

Patti: Thanks Dad.

Patti's skill at active listening, calmed her dad's anger, took the blame off of her and dad came up with a solution.

Jeff's Plans

Remember Jeff, the Jock from our opening chapter? Here is a way he used active listening to help in his relationship with his mom.

Jeff: "Mom, what you think about me joining the army? — **Conversation starter with an open ended question**

Mom: I think there are good opportunities for you because they will pay for college after your service but I'm afraid.

Jeff: "So, you are afraid for me? **Active listening, reflection of feeling**

Mom: "Yes, I'm afraid, you'll be hurt or worse. I'm sorry, your dad and I couldn't make another way for you to go to college. That's why you are going into the military."

Jeff: "You think payment for college is the reason I'm going into the military." **Active listening, reflection of meaning**

Mom: "Yes, it makes me sad. —**Confirmation of meaning**

There's a pause in the conversation. Then Jeff uses an I-Message to clarify and

personalize his meaning. (*I-Messages will be covered in the next chapter.*)

Jeff: "Mom, Grandpa understood. This is part of my heritage. I'm not doing this for college. That's a benefit. I'm doing this for me. It's part of what I want to do with my life.

Here is Kim's active listening sample. Kim is our punk rocker who feels misunderstood and disconnected from her family including her stepparents. Kim feels she needs to stand up for herself and the type of clothing she wears. Her stepmother wants a "pretty" picture at her biological daughter's (Kim's stepsister) wedding.

Check out the first conversation **without** Active Listening and I-Messages, then check out the conversation **with** those skills. Kim has a better shot at getting what she wants which is to remain true to herself using active listening and I-Message. She certainly has a better opportunity for peaceful relating and relationship building by using the effective communication skills.

Kim's Clothes Battle

Stepmom: So, what were you thinking of wearing to Emily's wedding?

Kim: I want to wear that simple black dress you bought me last fall. I can accessorize it.

Stepmom: No! You don't wear black to a daytime wedding. I know you! You will want to wear combat boots with it.

Kim: Yes and black nail polish and dark eye and lip make up (with a sarcastic tone).

Stepmom: No! I forbid it. Wait till your father hears about this.

Kim: Fine. I just won't go.

Clothes, Invite and Open Mindedness

Here's a similar conversation when Kim remembered to use active listening skills and I-Messages while keeping herself calm. Notice that it's a deeper conversation that requires each person try to hear and respect the perspective of the other.

Stepmom: So, what were you thinking of wearing to Emily's wedding?

Kim: I thought I would wear that black dress you bought me last fall and accessorize it.

Stepmom: Most etiquette books say that black for a daytime wedding isn't appropriate. Would you mind if I took you shopping so we can find something appropriate?

Kim: So, you want to take me shopping because you don't want me to embarrass you? **Active Listening and asking about meaning**

Stepmom: No. I want to take you shopping because you need something new. You have grown since we went shopping last. **Clarification of Meaning**

Kim: I'm happy to go shopping with you. Thank you. But I don't think we will agree about what's appropriate. I feel disrespected when you "dis" my style. **I-Messages**

Stepmom: I don't disrespect you Kim. We just sometimes don't agree about the appropriateness of your style. We will never know about a compromise dress if we don't go shopping and take a look at what's out there. Let's keep an open mind and try to find something that works for both of us.

Kim: Okay.

Myra's Mistake

Remember Myra, our popular girl from Chapter 1. She felt discounted by her parents and wished they believed in her. Instead of confronting it directly with them or working hard to make her dreams a reality anyway, she snuck around behind their backs to see her friends and the guys she was interested in. This conversation involves Myra's mom confronting her. In it Myra uses active listening to diffuse her mom's anger and disappointment in hopes of working out a solution together.

Mom: Myra, I called Maria's mom to find out about your group date last night since you and I "didn't have a chance to talk" and she said she didn't know anything about it.

Myra was angry her mom didn't trust her and checked up on her. She was afraid she had been found out in a lie. Instead of being defensive, she decided to keep her cool and use active listening, to try to help her mom feel heard

Myra: So she didn't know anything about it? **Active Listening - Rephrasing**

Mom: That's right. I don't understand why you would lie to me about a group outing when you were really out with Sam, your boyfriend.

Myra: You don't understand why I would lie to you. **Active Listening — Reflection of Meaning**

Mom: That's right I don't understand why you lied. **Confirmation of Meaning**

Myra: Mom, I'm sorry I lied. I should not have lied because I should talk to you directly about what I'm feeling. I'm 17 years old. In one year I will be an adult. I need to be making more independent

decisions about my own schedule and who I choose to spend time with. *I-Messages*

Angry Mom: As long as you live under my roof, young lady, you will abide by my rules. I need to know where you are going and I need to know who you are with! And you come home when I tell you.

*Myra: So, you are angry that I don't want to follow your rules. **Active Listening — Reflection of Feeling***

Mom: Yes, I'm angry! You don't respect my role as your mother!

*Myra: You feel disrespected. **Active Listening — Reflection of Feeling***

Mom: Yes! Stop, repeating everything I say.

*Myra: I learned this listening technique to build a better relationship with you. I want you to know I understand what you are saying and feeling. I want you to understand, that I'm almost an adult and I feel disrespected that you don't trust me to make good decisions. **I — Messages***

Mom: I want you to be safe. I'm scared for you. I don't want you to turn out like me.

*Myra: You are scared? **Active Listening — Reflection of Feeling***

Mom: Yes, I'm scared. I got pregnant at seventeen and even though it was one of the greatest blessings of my life, I didn't get to go to college or have a career.

Myra: You want me to be safe. **Active Listening and Confirmation of Feeling**

Mom: Yes.

Myra: Wow Mom! You never told me you wanted me to go to college and have a career. I'm really glad you said it. I understand you want me to be safe. I am being safe. **I-Messages**

Joe's Chore

Joe, our artist started a new job working at a grocery store bagging groceries and stocking shelves. Mom wants help with the housework on Saturday but Joe is wiped out from working afterschool all weeklong. Saturday is his only day to sleep late. His mom wants to clean house and do laundry on Saturday which is her day off also. Her idea is to get the chores done quickly so she can relax. Joe was willing to help but wanted to sleep late Saturday morning first. Mom kicks off the conversation with an I-Message. Joe remembers to use Active Listening to help his mom feel heard first before he makes his request.

Here's how the conversation might have gone before Joe learned the teen communication technique.

Saturday Morning

Mom: Joe, time to get up. Let's get busy! You said you would do floors for me.

Joe: Mom! Its 8:30 a.m.

Mom: Yeah, I know I was nice. I let you sleep half an hour late.

Joe: Mom! This is my only day to sleep. I told you I would do it. I will.

Friday night:

Mom: I want to get the chores done Saturday so I can rest and go to church on Sunday.
Joe: So you want the chores done on Saturday?
Active Listening — Checking Out Meaning

Mom: Yes. You said you would sweep and mop the floors.

Joe: Yes, I said I would do the floors. ***Active Listening and Affirmation***

Joe: Mom, does it matter when I do the floors? Or can it be done anytime this weekend? I'm really tired since I started my new job and Saturday morning is the only day to sleep. **Open ended questions with I-Message**

Mom: Okay. As long as the floors are done before dinnertime Saturday, I'm happy.

We have reviewed some conversations between our teens and their parents. These conversations are ideal and real life is messy. Nevertheless, active listening can work and empower you as a teen. Like most skills it takes practice to get good at it over time. If you practice it with your parents and friends with the small things at first over a meal at the dinner table or driving in the car on your way to school, you may just begin to see a difference in the way your parents relate to you. Active listening has a way of softening the person being heard over time. Building a better relationship with your parents makes everyone's life easier.

Exercise C — Active Listening

Think about the last problem your parent had with you or the last lecture they gave you. Could active listening have helped them feel heard and helped you both move to a solution more quickly? Write down their problem statement from their perspective and then write down your reflection of the last phrase they used. Do this to practice your skill in developing active listening and then try it on a friend in a real conversation for practice.

Parent Problem Statement:

_____

_____

Your active listening reflection of the last phrase used:

_____

_____

Chapter 5 - How to Talk So Your Parents Will Listen

We have talked about ways to build a new, positive relationship with your parents. One based on mutual respect that honors each other's perspectives and roles, not as right or wrong but as simply different. We have reviewed communication strategies such as problem definition and active listening. But you have a lot to say too.

This chapter will examine ways to speak to your parents that offer the best opportunity for them to truly "hear" you. The two strategies are, Open Ended Questions and I-Messages. We will start with Open Ended Questions because it is a great way to introduce a topic, even one that may be conflictual.

Open Ended Questions

Open ended, but specific questions can be conversation starters. Specific open ended questions cannot be answered with a one-word response like "yes" or "no." They invite more discussion. Open ended questions can also be used to open a conversation to find out where your parents stand on a subject or to make a "soft" opening to a difficult subject. Open ended questions can be followed up with Active Listening or I-Messages.

Open ended questions, don't direct the person being interviewed to answer any specific way. Each question is about a specific area of parent- teen life and has a sample follow up question. As you practice open ended question, listen and learn. You will find that you will develop your own conversation starters and tough topic openers that give you an opportunity to share your perspective later.

The following are examples of effective, specific open ended questions that help you get to know your parents and their perspective.

Sample Open Ended Questions for Relationship Building ONLY

Work

1.) What did you do at work today dad?

2.) What's your favorite part of work?

3.) What's your least favorite part of work?

Tip: Remember the point of this exercise is to get to know your parents as people, not just as your mom or dad. These open ended questions show genuine interest, beyond the question, *"How was work today?"* Be sure to ask at a relaxed time and show you really care. Don't ask in an effort to butter them up for when you want to ask for money or a privilege.

Leisure Time or Hobbies

4.) Mom what do YOU want to do this weekend?

a.) Is there something you would like to do if you had alone time this weekend?

5.) Tell me why you like to garden? It seems boring to me.

a.) Tell me when you became interested in football?

6.)What's your favorite thing about the weekends?

Tip: Sharing interests can be fun. You really earn credibility as being interested in their world. Go ahead! You can do it! One of my daughters open ended questions led to a discussion about our musical tastes. Now, on trips we take the opportunity to educate each other on the music we each like. We listen to one of her songs and then we listen to one of mine. She even attended a concert with me. Now, I have to return the favor.

Personal Development, Health or Spirituality

7.) I have been trying to meditate, how do you best re-charge your batteries after a stressful day at work?

8.) I have been working on a eating more vegetables, do you have a health goal?

9.) What do you think about working out together as a family?

Practice

If it feels awkward, try again. Then next time you are alone together, try again. Relationship building is hard work and it takes practice over time.

Tip: Ask these questions casually. Driving in the car on the way to or from school might be a good time to talk and get to know each other as people better.

Sample Open Ended Questions

To Start Conversations about Troubling Topics

Spring Break Plans

Teen kicks off the discussion with an Open Ended Question

You: Mom, what are your thoughts about a teen spring break trip with friends?

Mom: If there is an adult chaperone that I trust, I have no problem with it. Why? Are you and Chloe and the gang thinking about a trip?

You: Yeah, just thinking about it right now. We would have to start working hard and saving money this fall in order to be ready by the spring. Plus we need to find out what Chloe's parents think about it.

Debriefing: Rather than feeling shot down, you have discovered what the parameters are for mom feeling comfortable with it. If you and Chloe plan well, you might have a shot at getting what you want.

Responsible Drinking

Teen gives the background to the issue and then asks an Open Ended Question

You: In government class, we were talking about adulthood. You can vote at 18 years old and you can die for your country at 18 years old but you can't make a responsible choice about drinking until you are 21 years old in this state. Do you think that's right?

Mom: It does seem rather incongruent, doesn't it? When I was your age, I didn't think it was right. Now that I see so many teenage car accidents with alcohol involved, I feel differently.

You: We were also talking about the fact that your parents can serve you alcohol at home at any age in our state but you cannot order it on your own even when you are 18 years old. How do you feel about that?

Smart Mom: Are you thinking about going to a party where alcohol is served?

You: Yes. And I want credit for the fact that I'm talking to you about it and not hiding it. I also want you to remember that I'm just thinking about it.

Mom: I appreciate your maturity and the very adult way you are conducting this conversation with me. I'm impressed. Please give me the details...

I-Messages

Our final and most powerful communication tool is the I-Message. I-Messages are a meaningful and effective way of communicating your feelings and sharing your perspective. ***I-Messages work best when you have done the relationship building work with your parents first.***

I-Messages I-Messages communicate feelings about a behavior as non-judgmentally as possible without dictating terms. The purpose of I-Messages is to communicate your feelings and perspective effectively. Whatever the issue is between you and your parents, when you respond with how you feel about it, they cannot deny it. Your feelings and your perspective are yours. They have no morality meaning, they are neither right nor wrong.

Speaking from a feelings perspective or from your heart has a way of drawing out compassion for your perspective. Your parents may not agree with you on a subject, but they will likely be compassionate if you share your feelings. From there, you can co-create a solution that works for both you and your parents.

I-Message Formula:

I feel _____
(insert your feeling)
about _____ (your behavior or perspective).

Examples of I-Messages are:

- I feel trusted when you open up to me.
- I'm disappointed that you will work late and not make it to my band concert.
- I'm frustrated with my bad test grade because I asked for help and tutoring on more than one occasion.

Warning: A common mistake is to share thoughts in the I-Message format. If you share a thought, it's just an opinion and doesn't carry the personal power that a feeling does. You have likely heard, "everyone has an opinion," which is true. Opinions can be reasoned away. Feelings cannot be argued with. Your feelings are your feelings and they simply reflect your perspective which is likely different than that of your parents. Remember the aim of I-Messages is to effectively communicate your reality so that together you and your parents can work on solutions to situations or problems.

Sometimes teens lack the feeling labels for their emotions and simply say, "I feel good" or "I feel bad." Using specific words for emotions helps your parents better identify with what you are feeling. Here's a list of feeling words that you can use for your I-Messages.

Feelings List

GLAD	SAD	MAD	AFRAID
content	blah	angry	scared
pleased	hurt	annoyed	timid
playful	blue	grumpy	startled
cheerful	depressed	grouchy	fearful
calm	unhappy	disgusted	uncomfortable
safe	empty	impatient	tense
relaxed	lonely	hot	anxious
confident	disappointed	frustrated	worried
delighted	awful	bugged	frightened
happy	miserable	infuriated	disturbed
joyful	crushed	furious	shaken
loved	unloved	enraged	concerned
wonderful	down	destructive	terrified
terrific	heartbroken	irate	petrified

Practicing these skills may seem awkward or mechanical at first, but keep at it. You are practicing skills that will help you later in life when you need to tell your perspective to your significant other, spouse, boss or employees.

Patti

Here's Patti's powerful I-Message to her mom. She begins with an Open Ended Question to enter the potentially explosive topic. She waited until a Saturday morning when her mom woke up sober. She knew better than to talk to her mom when she was drunk.

Patti: Mom, how have you been feeling lately?
Open Ended Question

Mom: I'm okay. Why do you ask?

Patti: I feel scared for your health when you get drunk almost every day. I'm concerned about you.

Mom: Oh, Patti, don't start. I just woke up.

Patti: Exactly, Mom. Mornings are the only time I can talk to you.

Notice in Sara's conversation, how she asks for what she wants because she suspects how her mom will react and she wants to state her solution before the reaction. Then notice how she actively listens to calm her mom and assure her mom that she hears her concerns. Finally, notice Sara's 2 I-Messages one right after the other. This shows her mom how serious Sara is about her solutions because naming her emotions make an impact.

Sara

Sara: *Do you have time to talk?*

Mom: *Yes.*

Sara: *I want to tell you about a problem I have. I already have a solution but it requires your permission. Please hear me out all the way to the end before you share your ideas. Is that okay?*

Mom: *Yes, but I'm thinking this is bad.*

Sara: *I hear that you are suspicious and maybe afraid.* **Active Listening — Reflection of Feeling**

Sara continues: *But please just chill and give me a chance to finish. It's no secret that math is not my best subject. Despite my best efforts with tutoring and lots of studying I'm flunking.*

Mom: *What?*

Sara: *Mom, you promised to hear me out.*

Mom: *Okay.*

Sara: *Even if I magically starting "getting it," it's just too late to pass the semester. So, I talked to the* teacher. He is willing to give me a "drop-pass" if I get out now. I can take an easy computer course for an elective credit and then start again, next semester on algebra. The counselor said, it would be better for my grade point average, which in the long run might be better for college acceptance. I'm disappointed that I am failing. **I-Message 1**

Sara: But given the situation, dropping the class with a re-boot next semester may be the best solution for me. I feel responsible for dealing with the situation.

I — Message 2

Mom: I don't like this Sara. I think we should have started tutoring much sooner in the semester. But given where you are now and because you have done the research to find a solution and you are not giving up on algebra, just delaying the coursework, I support you.

Sara: Oh, thanks mom. Will you help me talk to dad?

Sam uses all the communication skills despite being in a very stressful situation. His honesty helps his father soften and identify with him and it ultimately helps them come to several solutions together.

Sam

Sam is in trouble again. This time he went to the principal's office for a prank. Sam's dad is angry. He works offshore in the oil industry so he doesn't see Sam often. Even though Sam's dad doesn't live with him, he tries to keep up with Sam's life.

Dad: What happened this time Sam? **Open-ended question**
Sam: It was just a prank Dad and I wasn't the only one.

Dad: I try to provide for you, son and this is how you repay me? You have a chance to graduate high school and stay out of the oil field. You can be the boss, son, but you have to use your leadership skills for good!

Sam: I know you are disappointed. **Active Listening — Reflection of Feeling**

Dad: Yes, I'm disappointed! I don't want to be disappointed anymore Sal. You have too much potential. What do we need to do differently with you?

Sam: I understand you are really disappointed and want me to live up to my potential. **Active Listening — Reflection of Feeling**

Dad: That's right, but I need to hear from you about what YOU are going to do differently.

Sam: Dad, I'm disappointed too. In fact, I'm angry. I have done plenty of things wrong through the years, but this time I didn't. I have been in trouble so much in the past that the teachers automatically think I'm the one that starts the joke and disrupts class. Honestly, I used to do it dad. But since I started playing ball, I'm trying to think about my future. I've tried really hard to focus in class and just do my work. Talk to my best friend, Mike, I really didn't start this one dad. **I - Messages**

Dad: What are YOU going to do to fix this, Sam? I think they are talking about in school suspension.

Sam: If I'm suspended, then I can't play in the next game. I want to talk to the teacher, tell her what happened and see if there is anything I can do to change her mind and make it right. I'm willing to do almost anything. Are you willing to go with me dad?

Dad: Okay, son.

Sam: Dad, I need to talk about something else while we are getting along so well.

Dad: Okay, what is it?

Sam: It's Mom. She's not well. She needs help. She has crying spells and sometimes gets violent. With Monique (Sam's sister) married and out of the house and you separated from mom and offshore,

I'm the one left to deal with it. I feel almost abandoned and alone, man. **I-Message**

Dad: Okay, son. I'll try to get her some help.

You have read a few examples of conversations with active listening, open ended questions and I-Messages to better communicate with parents in this chapter and the last. Practice to apply the technique to your conversations with your parents by using the following exercise.

Exercise D — I Messages

Now it's your turn to try it. Think about a problem for you and your parents. Write a script where you open the conversation with an open ended question inviting their opinion about a topic, you actively listening to their perspective and then you use an I-Message to share your perspective. The purpose of this exercise is not to come to write a solution but to practice the communication skills outlined.

Your Opening Open Ended Question:
    How do you feel about? _____
                    (fill in the blank, restating the issue)

Parent:

I feel or I think _____

You:

I hear you saying_____

(use the last few words to reflect the thought or reflect the feeling underlying the words they use).

Parent: (Answers) yes or no.

Your I-Message: I feel _____

(use a feeling word; see the list)

when you do_____
(name your parent's behavior or attitude that bothers you)

Your Closing Open Ended Question: Can we come up with a solution together?

Tip: Memorize this conversation format. Practice it with different topics with your friends and family.

The ability to Actively Listen, ask Open-Ended Questions and state I-Messages will not only help you gain more independence, share power and have a better, more positive relationship with your parents, it will also help you speak to persons in authority anywhere, a teacher, an administrator or an employer. Adults who use these skills in the workplace are seen as trustworthy leaders.

Chapter 6 — Do You Have Skills? How to Handle Hot Button Issues

The Best Conditions to Practice Your Skills

Seeing your parents as non-judgmentally as possible while learning to communicate with them effectively can help you co-create a positive relationship with them. Watching for or asking for relationship building opportunities such as fun activities, learning new skills together, problem solving or asking for help in crisis can help you feel closer to your parents and grow trust.

Learning communication skills to share your perspective confidently such as active listening, open-ended questions and I-messages can help you share the decision making power in your relationship with your parents which prepares you for relationships you will have as an adult.

Knowing when and how to engage your parents in co-creating a new relationship is important. For example, when they are tired or stressed isn't the best time to have a conversation. When you need to confront them with some bad news or discuss a difficult topic that may require a decision its best to look for the right time. A good rule of thumb is to wait to discuss things if they are hunger, angry, lonely or tired. A good way to remember these conditions is the acrostic HALT.

Hungry
Angry
Lonely
Tired

The same holds true for you. Don't expect to practice your new communication skills well if you are hungry, angry, lonely or tired.

Reptile Brain: The Old Fight or Flight Mechanism

No. Your parents aren't reptiles but like you, they have instinctual reactions to things when they feel threatened. Some parents are really calm and don't get worked up easily and other parents almost live in a state of high alert. Medical doctors and psychologists call this the flight fright mechanism. Be alert to the fact that when you share your perspective and discuss things that they may disagree with, they may go quickly to that instinctual fight or flight mechanism depending on their brain chemistry and personality reactions. Choose the time you talk careful and if the defense mechanism is engaged, **simply take a break**.

How will you know if your parent is defensive or stressed?

- Excessive sweating, talking, twitching
- Talking fast
- Going silent
- Yelling back

• Extra tension in the face and/or other body parts

Taking Breaks from Communicating

You have the right to come back to a discussion later. It will demonstrate your maturity to intervene and not allow your emotions (or theirs) to escalate out of control or resort to yelling. Read your parents' body language and say something like this.

"Mom, this discussion is stressful, let's take a break and come back to it later."

"Dad, I don't want to fight with you about this. Let's take a break and talk tomorrow. Nothing has to be decided today."

Notes and Letters

Unfortunately, some topics are too hot to handle. Some teens have elected to write letters to their parents about conflictual topics such as health, friends, the potential for substance abuse, school grades and more. A good rule of thumb is to keep the letter to one page only. Use a similar format to what you would use in conversation.

Suggested Template of a Letter to Avoid Conflict

Dear Mom and Dad:

I would like to know your feelings on the

_____ *(name the subject).*

I feel _____ *about*

_____ .

I suggest _____ *(a mutually*

beneficially solution.)

End by thanking them for trying to work this out with you.

Love,
Your Name

How to Grow Your Parents' Trust in You

a.) Start Small — Be Patient

Some change in your relationship with your parents when you desire it is better than no change. Start by active listening this afternoon. Work hard and craft one I-Message about an issue that is bothering you. Give yourself a pat on the back for having started a new relationship with your parents.

b.) Own Your Growth and Your Mistakes Nobody is perfect!

Your teen years is the time in your life to experiment with new behaviors, new friends and new activities. By definition that means you will make mistakes. That's okay. It's part of the process. Sometimes the adults in your life will forget that. It's okay to respectfully remind them.

Mom, you're right I messed up. I forgot to feed the dog. I will get better. I just need to get my backpack ready before I go to bed the night before so I'm not rushing around in the morning and can slow down and remember what I need to do before I walk out of the door.

Dad, you're right I forgot to fill up the car with gas before I came home. I'll get better.

When you make a mistake own it. Make a commitment to try to improve.

c.) Know the Difference Between a Request and a Demand

No one likes to be told what to do and no one likes to be controlled.

The first time we tell our parents, "no," during our terrible twos, we are either confronted with threats, "oh yes, you will," or distracted with another toy or activity because our little attention spans are too short. But we said "no" for a reason. "No" is the first step towards independence.

The whole purpose of the parenting is to help you grow and prepare for the future. One of the ways you grow is to learn to express your likes and dislikes. To do so **tactfully and respectfully** is a skill you will need in adulthood. Practice it with your parents.

Sample Respectful Requests

I like_____. May I go get it? May I have some?

I prefer we do this activity later.

I want to do the following:

_____ What do you want to do?

I respectfully disagree. What if we tried this instead, _____
(name your suggested solution or option).

I prefer waiting. Let me think about that.

d.) Pick Your Mentors

One of the best things a parent can do for a child is to provide access and relationships with other safe adults that will keep the child's confidentiality but maintain similar values as the child. Sometimes these mentors can be aunts, uncles, adult cousins or friends of the family who are easily available to you. Other times, families in distress are isolated and don't have access to extended family members or church leaders.

Teens often need an objective ear to hear their perspective. Teens can find their own adult mentors. A good mentor is: 1) a caring adult, 2) who is readily available for quick but meaningful conversations. Adults that often meet these criteria are teachers, coaches or church leaders.

A positive strategy with worried parents that are having trouble letting go, is to simply tell your parent that you will or have had a conversation about a troubling issue with your mentor and name that mentor to them. It may help your parents relax.

My friend and former neighbor Bobby moved to L.A. to pursue a career as a musician, actor, and production support specialist. He has acted in major motion pictures and television shows and sung with major recording artists. Every year around the holidays, he visits his mother. Last trip he was home, I introduced him to my daughter, Grace. Despite their age difference, they have similar tastes in music. While working on the FUSE TV camera crew at Warped Tour L.A., he sent her updates with pics and quotes every few hours. They really hit it off! He has become a trusted mentor to her. When we had a family problem, Grace reached out to him. I feel comforted and confident that Grace has a positive role model in her life. I am more willing to stay out of her business and trust her judgment because she is connected to a person I trust.

e.) Introduce Your Friends

A positive way to build trust with your parents is to be open and introduce your parents to your friends. The hope is, if they know your friends, they will see they can trust your values. Then they may be more readily willing to trust you in other things.

There's a risk in introducing your parents to your friends. They might not like them! If this happens. Actively listen to your parent's perspective and then use your I-Messages.

I hear you Mom. Ashley is a little wild and dresses like a goth. **Active Listening**

But I like her. She is a loyal friend and she is really smart.

When you criticize my friends, I feel disrespected as if you don't trust my judgment. I — **Message**

This is my chance to learn who I like and why, so I will have good judgment when I choose friends in college.

f.) Self-Regulate: Internet, Dating and Homework

Self-regulation is simply self-discipline. No one is perfect at it. The only way to learn what disciplines work for you in your family situation is to experiment, make mistakes, learn lessons and try again. That's exactly how we grow and learn.

• If you stay up too late on a school night, playing video games, you won't feel well in school the next day.

• If you date the good looking, popular kid in school but they put you down, don't go out with them again, even if it makes life easier at school for a while. Those kind of pay offs are temporary.

- If you don't study for your math test, you won't get a good grade and you might risk repeating the course the next semester.

All of these are scenarios for learning self-discipline. The lessons learned in these scenarios are lessons that can be transferred to adulthood with preparing for work.

Share your lessons with your parents. Take a risk and share what you are learning with your parents. By showing your parents that you are learning and growing you can build trust. With some more controlling parents, you might risk a lecture. But all you have to do is simply say, "*Yes, I learned that lesson.*" You might also get a pat on the back for learning and growing. Either way, you will know that you are growing up and you will have demonstrated maturity.

g.) Prioritize: Balance School and Fun

Teen lives can be so structured these days. It seems teens have to keep very regimented schedules in order to keep up with school, extra-curricular activities, friends and family, as if every hour of the day is filled with something. Sometimes if feels as if you don't have time to yourself. It is important to work towards balance.

- Balance between time alone and time with friends and family.
- Balance between school work and fun.
- Balance between a hobby, sport or extracurricular activity and "down" time, alone or with friends.

Learning balance can be difficult in our society where every waking minute is spent with some stimulation or electronic device. Balance is a goal that your parents are striving for also. Perhaps you can discuss with them ways that you can both slow down for yourselves and for each other.

h.) Explore your Truth

There is a lot of information about healthy eating, the importance of exercise, mental agility and even emotional well-being. We live in an age of self-improvement and selfies. There is another dimension of growth besides physical, mental, emotional, social or financial. It is the spiritual dimension.

Your parents may have raised you in a church, synagogue or mosque. The teen years is the time of your life when you begin to question what you have been given and find your own path. It may be the same religious path your parents introduced or it may be something different. Spirituality is the belief and practice of something larger than yourself. You can be spiritual **without** being religious and you can be spiritual **and** religious. *The choice is yours.*

Just don't neglect it. Some ways to discover your own spirituality and truth are:

- Silence
- Prayer
- Meditation
- Chanting
- Listening to music that settles your soul
- Discovering Nature
- Journaling
- Yoga
- Poetry
- The Practice of Gratitude
- The Practice of Service
- Volunteering
- Fasting for short periods of time
- Reading spiritual literature
- Church attendance
- Talking to friends and trusted advisors about spiritual things

If you are feeling brave and adventurous, share your discoveries about your spirituality with your parents. Use the co-creation communication skills. Remember to respect difference.

Chapter 7: What If?

What if my parent abuses alcohol or drugs?

Our teen, Patti was dealing with a parent that had a substance abuse problem.

Take Care of Yourself First

When you are flying in an airplane, before take-off the flight attendant will tell you in the safety talk if you are traveling with a child if there is a loss of cabin pressure (if the plane is going down) put your mask on first, then put the mask on the child. Why? You cannot help anyone if you are unconscious. The same holds true for this very serious issue of alcohol or drug abuse.

If your parent is abusing alcohol or drugs, first know that you are not alone. Approximately 25% of families in the United States suffer from alcoholism, drug addiction or mental illness in a one of their direct family members, in their household. Like Patti's story in the beginning of the book, you may live with a stressful unpredictability that may have worsened over time so gradually that you don't even realize that you are living in crisis. Crisis living strains our bodies, minds and souls.

Kids of alcohols learn to not talk about their lives. They don't talk about their feelings or thoughts. In fact, children of alcoholics may not even know what they feel. They may have lived in unpredictable crisis for so long that their emotions are frozen or numb. As a result, children of alcoholics are distrustful. Without help or intervention, children of alcoholics have an 80% chance of growing up to be alcoholic themselves or marry someone with a compulsive addictive personality. So, if you are growing up with alcoholic or addicted parents, get help for yourself, first!

The good news is, recovery from the effects of a parents' drinking or using, can happen when children of alcoholics begin to trust others enough to talk about what is going on and actually fully feel their feelings. One of the best places to begin the journey of recovery is the self-help support groups of Alateen and Al-Anon. These are the sister organizations to Alcoholics Anonymous. They follow a simple 12-Step Model of Recovery and use a support group dynamic to help each other. There is no cost. Look up Alateen or Al-Anon online and find the meeting nearest you.

How to Help Your Parent

The American Medical Association has defined alcoholism and addiction as diseases which are physical, mental, emotional, spiritual and volitional (affecting their will or ability to choose). The number one symptom is denial. It is the one disease that tells you, you don't have it and you don't need treatment. The most popular treatment or intervention is the self help support groups of

Alcoholics Anonymous. They are located all over the world, most likely in your town too.

You can find a meeting near you by looking up Alcoholics Anonymous, (type your town name) or call directory assistance or ask a police officer. Alcoholics Anonymous meetings are for the identified problem drinker. The person does not have to talk and does not have to call themselves alcoholic in order to attend. (The same process is true for people with addictions. They may attend Narcotics Anonymous or Cocaine Anonymous.)

The most frequently asked question by teens about parents with a drinking problem or an addiction is, how do I get them to go? The answer, practice your own recovery! Remember children of alcoholics don't talk, trust or feel. So, for your recovery you must feel your own feelings of hurt, betrayal, anger or disappointment and risk telling your parent about them. No one can argue with your own feelings. They are yours. They are your reality.

Sometimes it's helpful to talk to your non-alcoholic parent and attend Al-Anon first. Remember your drinking or using parent is ill. They are not bad. Use your support system, gather your strength, look up a meeting and ask your parent to attend. Talk about the elephant in the living room.

Get Help!

1.) Attend Alateen or Al-Anon or Co-Dependents Anonymous meetings near you. These self-help support groups have websites online with information about meetings near you. Ask a friend to go with you to your first meeting,

Alcoholics Anonymous www.aa.org and Alanon/ Alateen www.al-anon.org

2.) Talk to your family doctor, a trusted school counselor or teacher, a member of the clergy (priest, rabbi, minister) and get help for talking to your parent about their problem.

3.) Get counseling for yourself and your parent. The list of people in #2 can provide a referral.

What if my parent is depressed?

Our teen, Sal had this issue with his mom. She even abused him as a child.

Depression is more than just feeling sad or going through a tough time. It's a serious mental health condition that requires understanding, treatment and follow through. Some people may have only one episode of depression in a lifetime, but for most people depression recurs. Left untreated, depression can have life-threatening consequ-ences.

Symptoms, as listed by the NAMI, the National Alliance on Mental Illness

https://www.nami.org/

Just as true with any mental health condition, people with depression or who are going through a depressive episode (also known as major or clinical depression) experience symptoms differently. But for most people, depression changes how they function day-to-day.

- **Changes in sleep**. Many people have trouble falling asleep, staying asleep or sleeping much longer than they used to. Waking up early in the morning is common for people with major depression.

- **Changes in appetite**. Depression can lead to serious weight loss or gain when a person stops eating or uses food as a coping mechanism.

- **Lack of concentration**. A person may be unable to focus during severe depression. Even reading the newspaper or following the plot of a TV show can be difficult. It becomes harder to make decisions, big or small.

- **Loss of energy**. People with depression may feel profound fatigue, think slowly or be unable to perform normal daily routines.

- **Lack of interest**. People may lose interest in their usual activities or lose the capacity to experience pleasure. A person may have no desire to eat or have sex.

- **Low self-esteem**. During periods of depression, people dwell on losses or failures and feel excessive guilt and helplessness. Thoughts like

"I am a loser" or "the world is a terrible place" or "I don't want to be alive" can take over.

- **Hopelessness**. Depression can make a person feel that nothing good will ever happen. Suicidal thoughts often follow these kinds of negative thoughts — and need to be taken seriously.

- **Changes in movement**. People with depression may look physically depleted or they may be agitated. For example, a person may wake early in the morning and pace the floor for hours.

- **Physical aches and pains**. Instead of talking about their emotions or sadness, some people may complain about a headache or an upset stomach.

To be diagnosed with depression, a person must have experienced a major depressive episode that lasts longer than two weeks. The symptoms of a major depressive episode include:

- Loss of interest or loss of pleasure in all activities

- Change in appetite or weight

- Sleep disturbances

- Feeling agitated or feeling slowed down

- Fatigue

- Feelings of low self-worth, guilt or shortcomings

- Difficulty concentrating or making decisions

- Suicidal thoughts or intentions

Diagnosing depression can be complicated because a depressive episode can be part of bipolar disorder, another mental illness or substance abuse.

Get Help!

1.) Talk to your family doctor, a trusted school counselor or teacher, a member of the clergy (priest, rabbi, minister) and get help for talking to your parent about their problem.

2.) Get counseling for yourself and your parent. The list of people in #1 can provide a referral.

911

If your parent threatens suicide, take it seriously, call 911 immediately!

What if my parents are divorcing?

Our teens, Jeff, Joe and Myra had to deal with their parents' divorce.

About half the marriages in the United States today end in divorce, so plenty of kids and teens have to go through this. But when it happens to you, the pain can be overwhelming. You may feel insecure and afraid or you may cover it all with anger. Regardless of how you feel, it is how YOU feel. You will have a lot of feelings regarding the divorce. It is important to speak with another adult mentor or a counselor.

While the experience of divorce between parents may be similar to what your siblings or friends have gone through, your experience is uniquely your own. Whether you wanted it because the fighting in your house finally comes to an end or whether the divorce announcement took you by surprise, divorce is life changing for all involved. You can find support and move through it, but your path through it may not look like anyone else's path and that is perfectly, okay.

Keeping your feelings bottled up can lead to depression and acting out your problems with others at home or at school can only get you into trouble.

It is important to recognize what you are feeling so you can eventually resolve it.

What are some emotions I may feel after the divorce?

- **Shock** — especially if you were not expecting the divorce

- **Anger** — either directed at your parents or at no one specifically

- **Sadness** — you may feel like your family and part of your identity is gone

- **Guilt** — you feel like the divorce is your fault

- **Anxiety** — worrying about the future and who is going to take care of you

- **Worry** — you feel that in the future you will get divorced

- **Fear** — afraid of losing a parent

- **Embarrassed** — you do not want people to know that things in your family are changing

- **Loneliness** — no one understands you or understands what you are going through

- **Relief** — there is now less tension at home

- **Betrayed** — they didn't keep their promise to each other; you may feel now that they might not keep their promises to you

http://www.safeteens.org/relationships/dealing-with-divorce/ **and**
http://kidshealth.org/teen/your_mind/families/divorce.html#

It is critical to remember that you did not cause the divorce and you cannot fix it. Divorce is an adult problem, not a teen problem.

What helps make dealing with divorce easier?

• **Stay focused on you!** Sometimes a divorce can make you feel like you have to put your life on hold to deal with your parents' problems — but you need to live your life. The sooner you can create a sense of normalcy, the better for all. Keep doing what you love to do and if you need support, lean on your friends, other family members, trusted adults or seek professional help.

• **Focus on the positive.** Divorces happens for lots of reasons. They are adult reasons. The result of the divorce might mean that your parents are happier and maybe even have more time to spend with you. The quicker you can establish traditional family routines again, the better. You will also learn skills that help you handle tough circumstances and become stronger. This will help you be more resilient which will help with the crises of life as you grow older.

• **Don't worry about the future:** talk to your parents about your concerns. If you are worried that their divorce might ruin your future plans, let them know about it. They are still your parents. Together you can come up with solutions.

- **Be fair to both parents.** Don't take sides. Parents are hurting emotionally also and may try to manipulate you into taking sides. Try not to. Both parents made mistakes in the marriage. The one thing they did right was have you, provide for you and love you.
- **Stay in touch.** if you have to alternate time between your mom's house and your dad's house it can be hard on the other parent. Keep to the schedule but stay in phone contact with the other parent.

Get Help!

Let others support you. Talk about your feelings and reactions to the divorce can really help. If you're feeling down or upset, let your friends and family members support you. Your parents, school counselor, or a doctor or other health professional can help you find one. Sometimes, divorce can uncover a depression that you have been struggling to deal with for some time. Getting help can help you learn new coping skills that can make life easier in general. Some communities and schools have support groups for kids and teens whose parents have divorced. It can also help to talk with other people your age who are going through similar experiences.

What if my parents are remarrying or remarried and I have four parents to deal with?

Our teen, Kim was dealing with two remarriages in her family system.

Building a relationship with a stepparent is different than building other new relationships. You get to decide if you like them or not and you decide if you want to have a real relationship with them or not. You decide how big a role you want them to have in your life. But you don't have to decide right away. It is important to separate out the grief you may still feel about your parents' divorce and what you feel about having a stepparent.

Sometimes a stepparent can feel like a stranger who is suddenly thrown into some of the most personal aspects of your life. The pressure to get along can be intense. Take your time. Get to know this new person as a person first and not as a parental figure. For example, even when you like a new stepparent, it's natural to feel a little guilty that this new person is "replacing" your biological parent in some way. You may have all kinds of complicated feelings. Some of them may even be in conflict with each other.

These websites may be helpful.

http://kidshealth.org/teen/your_mind/families/stepparents.html or
http://teens.webmd.com/living-with-step-parent

Change is difficult. Even if you don't have negative feelings about the new person in your family, you may have very strong feelings about the changes a stepparent is creating. At some point, you're probably going to feel confused, conflicted about your loyalties, angry, and possibly sad.

Here are a couple of things to try that may help put your feelings into perspective.

- Keep a journal.

- Seek support from a friend.

- Talk to your parent or another trusted adult mentor about how you are feeling. Don't isolate.

- Stay focused on the good in your own life.

You can also talk to a teacher or a guidance counselor about what's going on in your life. Mental health professionals, such as social workers or therapists, are trained to help people sort out the conflicting mix of feelings that can accompany a parent's remarriage.

Dealing with a stepparent is like dealing with your parent if you are respectful and can disagree agreeably. Use the co-creation skills outlined in this book. Present your side — maybe you have to study for a test or you already made plans with friends and they're relying on you. Then listen to the other person's perspective. Include your parent in the discussion, too. If you're particularly mad about something, it can feel hard not to lose control. But managing your anger and taking extra care to choose respectful language will help your stepparent see you for the mature person you are, not as a child.

Expect some ups and downs. Building a good relationship takes time. Your new life won't always be smooth, so be ready to make some compromises. The good thing is, the highs and lows of adjusting to a new family situation can provide life lessons. Many people look back on their experience of getting to know new family members and realize they learned some great negotiating skills.

Chapter 8: Putting It All Together — Be True to Yourself

Above all else, be true to yourself.

Congratulations! If you have tried some of the skills in this book, you are on your way to taking charge of your life. Perhaps you have learned in a more conscious way, what you can do to influence your relationships.

By continuing to practice these skills with your parents, friends and other adult mentors in your life, including employers, you are learning to respectfully stand up for yourself and take your place in the world. No one does it perfectly. Being mature enough to ask for help when you need it, can help you get through the stressful times of growing up.

Using co-creation skills can be empowering. They can help you build the relationships you want to build with the adults in your life that are important to you and these skills can help you grow the kind of future you want.

Let's check in with the teens we profiled and see how using co-creation skills has improved their relationships with parents and helped them grow.

Patti

When Patti confronted her mother about her drinking, using I — Messages. She did so without any expectation of change. She just needed to speak her truth and be honest about not being able to carry the weight of the world, much less the house and farm on her shoulders. By being direct with her communication through I — Messages, she was actually able to begin to let go a little. She started to believe that she could not change or cure her mother's alcoholism even though she had compassion for her as she would for any sick person with a disease.

Patti's stepdad started taking her to Alateen when he went to his A.A. meetings.

Dad: Patti, I want you to go to the meeting with me tonight.

Patti: What? I don't have the problem. She does!

Dad: Actually, we all have the problem. Alcoholism is a family disease. I want you to go to the Alateen Family Group while I go to the A.A. Group.

Patti: I have enough to do! I'm behind on homework and chores.

Dad: I understand you feel behind (**Active Listening**)

Dad: But this is really important, not for your mom but for you. I really want you to go. (**I — Message**) *I'm asking you to go.*

Patti: So, this is really important to you? (**Active Listening**) *I don't think you have ever told me what you really wanted like this before. You usually deliver orders to me. Why is this important to you?* (**Open Ended Question for relat-ionship building**)

Dad: Because what your mother decides to do about her drinking is one thing but you have been affected too. You take the responsibility on yourself and try to be the adult. Its time you focused on yourself, on your own health and your own dreams.

Patti: But what will happen to her?

Dad: I don't know. But we'll get better and maybe in the long run that will help her. I don't say it often because I'm your stepparent and I'm a gruff SOB sometimes, but I do love you, Patti.

Patti: I love you too, Daddy.

Sounds a little too good to be true? Well, Patti's stepdad did genuinely care about her. He was working his own recovery program by being vulnerable and reaching out to Patti. Patti and her stepdad were never super close but they did reach a loving understanding. Patti trusted that he had her best interest at heart. She attended Alateen meetings and got to know the other teens in the group who were living with a parent's active alcoholism. She learned about the coping skills that helped these teens enjoy their lives. Two years later after Patti was in college Patti's mom finally got some help. She had a seizure due to alcohol poisoning one afternoon. It seemed to be the wake-up call she needed.

Myra

Myra, the beautiful but insecure cheerleader felt her parents didn't believe in her because their only dream for her was to graduate high school, marry and have a family. After Myra's mom found out that she sometimes snuck out of the house at night to go out with her friends, Myra had an opportunity to tell her how she really felt. Myra hoped that beginning to speak honestly about what she felt would help her mother see her differently.

But nothing really changed. Myra was disappointed and hurt at first. However with overtime and more conversations, Myra came to accept that her mom couldn't dream bigger for her because her mother had never experienced anything except being a wife and mother. Family was part of Myra's dreams too but she knew she wanted more. Besides being in cheerleading, she was also on the high school tennis team. Her brother was a tennis freak and had been coaching her on the side. She was a natural athlete and won several tournaments in singles. Her high school coach and brother secured a college scholarship offer in tennis. Selfishly Myra's boyfriend didn't want her to go and leave town.

Myra was scared and excited all at the same time. She didn't know what it would be like, but she decided she wanted to go. She was afraid her traditional parents might not be supportive. Her brother had gone to college and was studying kinesiology to be a coach. Myra's traditional parents were counting on Myra to stay close to home and help with the family business after graduation. If she wanted to go to college, they would support her. They just thought she would go to the local community college. Her tennis scholarship was with a four-year college upstate.

The conversation revealing her news and true feelings went something like this. She didn't think they would take it well.

Myra: Mom, Dad, graduation will be here before we know it. I know you were counting on me to help at the shop this summer and even after that. But I have an incredible opportunity. I have a tennis scholarship to a four-year college upstate. What do you think about that? **Open Ended Question**

Mom: What do you think? **Open Ended Question**

Myra: I love you both very much. I want to help at home and with the shop. But I want to start college there in the fall. I don't want to have regrets. **I - Messages**

Dad: I don't want you to leave and move away. I want to keep you at home forever. But I didn't raise my children to be afraid of life. If this is what you want for your future, you should go for it. **I - Messages**

Myra feared the worst. She lost sleep the night before this conversation. She was so afraid her parents' economic need and traditional ways would get in the way of her future, that she didn't sleep the night before. She forgot one critical piece of information. Her parents love her and want what's best for her.

Sometimes we can work ourselves up thinking we know all the factors involved and we anticipate the worst outcome. Parents can surprise us. In the end, parents do want what is best for their children.

Jeff

After Jeff had the conversation about joining the military before college with his mom recounted in Chapter 4, Jeff chose not to discuss it further. He never discussed his decision to delay college and go into the military with his dad. He simply went to his local recruiting office and signed up. He announced to both his parents at dinner one night. The remainder of the dinner was silent. There was a tearful good bye when he caught his bus to Fort Hood where he would take basic training, but there was no heartfelt discussion.

The military was good for Jeff. He liked the structure and felt proud to be a part of something larger than himself. Unfortunately, he was deployed to Afghanistan and suffered a loss of a limb. He would tell you, he was one of the lucky ones. He came out of the military an officer and the military paid for college. Decisions have consequences. If Jeff had communicated more effectively, he may have had the opportunity to discuss other options with his parents regarding college and his future plans. Military service is a noble thing and it may have been the right decision for Jeff, but we will never know what better communication and empowerment could have done in his life. Jeff married a lovely girl out of college but they divorced after 10 years in part because he struggled to talk about his feelings.

Kim

Kim practiced co-creation communication skills with her stepmother and was able to see some improvement but she still struggled to tell her biological parents what she really thought. Kim developed an anxiety disorder. She used music and her poetry to express herself, but she still felt isolated. One day at a routine doctors visit, the physician asked her to take off her bandana wrist bands for the examination. The doctor found cuts on her wrists and thighs. The examination disclosed that Kim had been cutting herself to deal with her feelings rather than communicate them. Kim and her mom went to therapy and improved their communication. Kim's mom learned to back off the demanding perfectionistic talk and Kim learned to open up a little more. Here's a sample of their conversation.

Mom: Kim, I'm really afraid for you. I don't like that dark music you listen to. I think it contributes to your depression and anxiety. **I - Messages**

Kim: Kim wanted to scream, its none of your freaking business! But she didn't. She took a deep breath and said with as much genuine compassion as she could muster, "So, you are really afraid for me?" **Active Listening and Summarizing Meaning**

Mom: Yes, Kim. I love you. (Mom looked as if she was going to cry.) **I - Message**

Kim: I'm sorry you are so scared about my depression and anxiety. I don't want to cause you pain or problems. Maybe if you listened to some of the lyrics with me, you would see that some of it really lifts me up. **I — Messages**

Mom: Okay

Sam

After getting out of jail overnight and having the charges reduced to a misdemeanor, Sam was suspended from school. The experienced served as a wake-up call. One of the coaches noticed his size and asked him to try out for football. He did and he loved it. Being a part of a group has really helped Sam have a sense of belonging. Despite being blamed for a prank, Sam was able to talk his way out of the school suspension with the help of his dad. His relationship with his dad improved but his mother's mental health steadily declined. Since he was a child, Sam had been a victim of her abuse whenever she went off her medication. Sam and his dad decided it was time for a change. Together with his sister, they found a program for Sam's mom. They took responsibility for her case management. It was decided since Sam's dad traveled for work, Sam would live with his adult sister. Sam was in agreement. He just wanted to make sure he could attend the same high school to play football. Here is an example of the conversations he has with his sister, Rosie.

Rosie: Sam, I am really proud of the way you have turned your life around. It's good to see you do well in school and get involved. **I-Messages**.

Sam: Thanks, sis.

Rosie: But I have to lay the law down because I have a child (Javier) myself now. Javi looks up to you. If you do anything to lead him astray, you are out of here. You know I love you, but he has to come first. If you drink again, go to jail or get in trouble with the law for any reason, that's it. I — **Messages and More**

Sam: You feel protective of Javi. **Active Listening**

You are a good mom. I feel protective of Javi too. I would never do anything to hurt him. I — **Messages**

Rosie: I wish I could have protected you when you were little Sam. I'm sorry.

Sam: It wasn't your job. And mom was sick. She doesn't even remember hurting me.

Joe

Joe expresses himself through his art. He isn't very keen on words. Applying the active listening skills and I-Messages has been a challenge. He found it awkward at first and thought about giving up. But he was also frustrated that he couldn't get his family to understand that art wasn't just his future, it was his life! So, he tried again.

Joe: Dad, why do you go hunting? **Open Ended Question**

Dad: I suppose I could say for the meat but the truth is I just love it. I like getting excited while I pack up for the trip the night before. I love traveling to the ranch. I love being outside. I enjoy reading the signs in the woods like animal tracks. Of course, I like making the kill.

Joe: Would you go hunting even if you didn't kill anything?

Dad: Yes, of course. I've done it plenty of times.

Joe: You are passionate about hunting. **Active Listening**

Dad: Yes, I guess so. I've never used that word, but yes, I am passionate about hunting. **Confirmation of Meaning**

Joe: Art is my passion, dad. If I never sell a painting or if I never go to art school, I will still paint. It's my passion. **I - Messages**

Dad: Okay. I can see that. But I want you to be able to take care of yourself. I want you to be able to make a living and take care of a family if you want to have a family. That's a man's responsibility.

Joe: I'll take care of myself dad. I will earn a living, take whatever jobs I have to, whatever it takes, but art is my life.

Joe had thought about how to make his dad understand that painting was like breathing to him. He wanted his dad to get it. He had a great idea to relate to his dad's passion for hunting. Joe used an open ended question to set up the conversation. You can script your side of the conversation, prior to having the conversation to help you get your meaning across or to keep calm if things become emotional. Remember, it's okay to take a break and try again later.

Closing

Co-creation attitudes and communication skills can help you do the work of growing into the young adult you want to be. The co-creation approach begins by defining who in the relationship has specific issues and builds to learn ways to listen and speak with adults in a way that helps them hear you better.

At the core of co-creation as an approach for relating to adults is empowerment. You and you alone have the power to change how you react to people, places and things. You also have the power to influence the relationships that are important to you.

You have the power to co-create the relationship you want with your parents.

Chapter 9 - Walk the Talk: Communicating at School and Work

Throughout this book, we have asserted that using communication skills to convey your attitudes and ideas to adults can give you the empowered independence to chart your own course in life. This kind of communication will influence how your parents and other adults see you. As you prepare for college, deal with counselors, administrators and financial aid officers, Active Listening, Summarizing, Open Ended Questions and I-Messages can help you communicate more effectively. As you enter the world of work and deal with office politics, co-workers and supervisors, the same communication skills will serve to clarify your views and help you show confidence and independence. These skills might even help you land a job or negotiate a raise! This chapter will show how the communication skills can be applied in school and at work.

You Get What You Give

The Golden Rule is about *treating others the way you want to be treated*. When we show others respect, they usually step up and respond in kind. When you clearly and respectfully express your thoughts, your feelings and your needs, you have a better chance of being treated with respect in all areas of your life.

Practicing the skills of active listening, summarizing for understanding, open ended questions and I-Messages prepares you to communicate with all the adults in your life not just your parents. This includes teachers, administrators, co-workers and bosses. By applying these skills consistently, you can demonstrate that you are ready to co-create the kind of respect you want.

The following teen–adult conversations deal with school and work situations. Teens use the communication skills and in so doing earn the respect of adults while taking full responsibility for their own lives.

Rule of Thumb

Active listening, Summarizing, Open-Ended Questioning and I-Messages can be helpful tools to express yourself, confront problems and defend against attacks whether they are real or perceived.

When using the skills with adults at school or work, a good rule of thumb to remember is, some skills are best when you are being confronted by someone to create space between you and the communicator, especially if the communication feels like an attack or a judgment against you. Other communication skills are best used when you want to assert your own thoughts, feelings or needs.

Think about football, when you play defense, the other team has the ball or the communication momentum. They are trying to drive their message home to the goal line. You play defense by slowing them down and choosing your actions rather than simply reacting to what they throw out there.

When you play offense in football you have the ball. You are the driving force in the communication. You are trying to get your message and meaning across the goal line.

Active Listening and Summarizing are more defensive tools that can be used when someone confronts you.

• Patti's situation below is somewhat defensive requiring the skills of active listening and summarizing. She creates emotional space for herself while formulating the message she wants to communicate.

Conversely, **Open Ended Questioning and I-Messages** tend to be used offensively or more pro-actively to express what you think, feel or need.

• Myra, Jeff and Kim have scenarios which require a little more interaction and are therefore more pro-active. These teens are the communication "ball-carriers" if we continue with the football metaphor. In both situations, the teens start by trying to communicate their messages.

Patti – Confronting an Immature Boss at Work

Patti went to work at a local pet store the summer between her junior and senior year. She loved working with the animals. She didn't mind taking inventory for her section of the store and she even enjoyed helping customers. But Patti didn't like the way her boss set up a competition between Patti and her co-worker, Sally. Patti was responsible for the cat food section and cat supplies and Sally was responsible for birds and bird supplies. Her boss Max, who was only 5 years older than Patti and Sally, thought the way to motivate his employees was to pit one against the other. The winner was the employee who sold the most but Patti was increasingly uncomfortable with the manipulative comments he would make telling one employee she was better than the other. Patti wasn't sure what to do. She talked to her best friend who reminded her that sharing her true feelings with respect worked well with her parents.

Patti's Work Conversation Example

Boss Max: Hey Patti, Sally's doing really well in the competition. Not only is she beating you, she's leading in sales because she sucks up more to the customers. You should be more like Sally.

Patti: So, you think I should "suck up" to customers? **Active Listening to Clarify Meaning**

Boss Max: Yeah! You know we have a video on customer service. Maybe you should listen to it.

Affirmation of Meaning

Patti: Thanks for the feedback and suggestion, Max. I appreciate healthy competition and your desire to motivate us, but manipulation doesn't motivate me. (*She worked on that line for 2 days and rehearsed it in the mirror.*) I always try to be courteous to everyone.

What Happens

Max didn't know what to say so he walked away. Patti's best friend and co-worker is Sally. Sally communicated something similar to Max about her feelings regarding the competition. After a few days Max dropped the competition and didn't hassle the girls anymore.

Myra: Asking for A Make Up Exam from a Teacher

Remember beautiful, popular Myra is our cheerleader. She has a high emotional intelligence factor which means she knows how to read people well, even adults. She hasn't been too good at communicating her real feelings, until recently. The truth worked well with her mom so the next time she had a need to communicate with an adult, this time, a teacher, she decided to try an I – Message.

In this example, Myra decides to lose the battle to get what she really wants which is to take a make-up exam.

Myra: Mr. Garcia I was absent last Friday because I had to get ready to cheer at the game so I need to take the make-up test. When is the best time to take it?

Mr. Garcia: Myra, I have told you at least 10 times that despite the fact you are excused for a school function, you need to set up the make-up exam before the event, not after. I told you that I don't mind if you test after the game, but you need to schedule the test with me before you leave.

Myra: You're right, Mr. Garcia. I forgot. I'm really sorry I disappointed you. It won't happen again. **I – Message Apology**

Myra decided this was a battle she could lose since she was going to be able to take the make-up exam anyway. In the old days, she might have batted her eyelashes and tried to talk him out of it. Since she started to take responsibility for herself, she was more willing to take the heat when she made a mistake.

Mr. Garcia: I've heard that before. To be sure you don't forget, I'm taking 10 points off your make-up exam.

Myra: I understand. Thank you, Mr. Garcia

What Happens

Myra takes the make-up exam and does her best to remember to inform her teachers about the need to do so ahead of time.

Jeff: Gives Notice of Resignation at His Job

Recall that, Jeff is our football player, wannabe ladies' man, tender-hearted senior who just joined the military so his college tuition would not burden his family. This conversation involves giving a two week notice to resign from his job at the mechanic's shop. First he tells the receptionist to soften the blow and get her support and then he tells the lead garage mechanic, his supervisor.

Jeff was working on a car with his boss when he decided to break the news. His boss Mr. Jones had been good to Jeff. He was flexible about scheduling, patient in teaching auto mechanics and treated Jeff more like a son than an employee. Jeff saw Mr. Jones as a mentor. Jeff didn't want to disappoint Mr. Jones by leaving abruptly or without showing his gratitude for all he had learned.

Mr. Jones: Pass me that wrench.

Jeff: This one? (Mr. Jones grunted, a yes.) I need to talk to you, sir.

Mr. Jones: Spit it out, we have a Mercedes coming in for a tune up later.

Jeff: I'm a little nervous. **I – Message**

Mr. Jones: You know by now, that I don't bite.

Jeff: I know. I know. I just don't want to disappoint you with a decision I've made.

Mr. Jones: This sounds important. I'm listening.

Mr. Jones pulled himself out from under the hood of the car he was working on and looked at Jeff directly.

Jeff: I've joined the Air Force. I leave in a month but I don't want to leave you short-handed in case you want to train a new guy.

And I want you to know how grateful I am for you and all I've learned from you.

I – Message

Jeff was proud of himself for getting it out the way he rehearsed it.

Mr. Jones: Son, how could I be disappointed by that? You are going to serve your country. You have a real talent with engines and I'd like to think I had a little part in shaping that.

Jeff: Oh you did, sir. That's why I want to work on planes now. Maybe even design something.

Mr. Jones: That's great! Let's go tell Jessica (the receptionist).

What Happens

Mr. Jones seemed so proud that Jeff didn't have the heart to tell him that he already told her.

Kim – Giving Notice at Work at a Job You Can't Stand

Not all resignations at work go as well as Jeff's. Kim worked at a fast food place after school. She was underpaid and undervalued. She decided to quit to focus on her studies and wait till summer to get another job. She told her supervisor Brenda that she needed to have a brief conversation after her shift. Brenda agreed to speak with her then.

Kim: I want to give you proper notice, I'm resigning.

Brenda: I'm sorry to hear that. You were doing well with order taking and on register. Why do you want to resign?

Kim: It would have been nice to hear something positive. All I hear is negative. I'm resigning because I feel bullied and disrespected on a regular basis. **I-Message**

Brenda: I didn't know you felt like that. I wish you would have spoken with me sooner.

Kim: Perhaps I should have, but I didn't trust you. I hope next time you hire someone that dresses differently than you or sounds differently than you, your team will not bully them. **I - Message**

Brenda seemed stunned by what Kim shared and by Kim's assertiveness.

What Happened

Kim was asked to turn in a two week notice of resignation in writing. Brenda must have spoken to the shift captains because everyone treated Kim with kid gloves, meaning they were awkwardly courteous to her over the next two weeks. Kim suspected it might be like that as she finished up. To Kim, it was almost worse than being bullied. All she ever wanted was to be treated like everyone else and not be singled out.

The most powerful thing about I-Messages is they communicate a feeling. The most powerful thing about feelings is, no one can argue with them. Your feelings are your feelings. Kim communicated her feelings based on her experience. She told her truth and decided that being true to herself meant she could not work in a place where she was disrespected.

Joe – Teacher Conference

This is a conference with Joe's teacher. The teacher confronted Joe about not paying attention in class. Joe had such success getting his dad to understand his passion for art, that he remembered that active listening and summarizing might work, rather than reacting negatively. The name of Joe's teacher is Mrs. Beck.

Mrs. Beck: Joe you are a bright student but your grades don't reflect that. What's going on?

Joe: So, this is about my bad grades? **Active Listening**

Mrs. Beck: Yes. I notice you drawing in class often and you don't pay attention. Something has to change, Joe or you will flunk this course, and I don't want to see that happen.

Joe: I'm sorry if that is a distraction or you think it's disrespectful for me to draw in class, but it actually helps me listen to you. Sometimes, I illustrate the literature you are lecturing about.

Mrs. Beck: Do you have college plans?

Joe: Yes, ma'am. I'm planning on going to the Art Institute in Chicago.

Mrs. Beck: That's wonderful. So, drawing is part of who you are and you need Senior English to graduate. We need to work with your talent; not fight with it.

Joe: How do we do that?

Mrs. Beck: You gave me an example of a visual and tactile learner. You need to see and touch in order to learn best. Why don't you cut the length of your required book report in half and submit an illustration that depicts the character development with it.

Joe: That's great Mrs. Beck! Thanks for understanding.

The conversations outlined may seem ideal. But they demonstrate how teens take full responsibility for their relationships but standing up for who they are with respectful but clear communication skills that earned them respect in turn.

Note that the teens exhibited the following.

- **Honesty** – Each teen is truthful about what they are feeling and what they want to express. Each is *courageous* for speaking their truth as they see it.

- **Willingness to Practice** – Most teens practiced their I-Messages in the mirror in advance of having their conversations. Sometimes, this included talking it out with a trusted, friend or advisor.

You are fully responsible for your side of your relationships. You have the power to communicate effectively and clearly about who you are and what you want and need.

Walking the Talk in Four Simple Steps

o   The next time an adult confronts you about your behavior or attitude, use active listening to create space for yourself and try not to react emotionally to what they say.

o   Summarize the meaning of what you think they are trying to say and ask them if that is correct. Let them clarify if necessary.

o   Think about what you want to communicate to them. Take your time. Don't be afraid to ask for a break. Use feeling words about what their behavior or communication prompts you to feel.

o   Then form a simple I-Message about what you feel and want.

I feel _____ (feeling word) about _____ (their behavior or attitude).

*If you need to confront something with an adult. Go directly to step #4 and use an I-Message, confidently. Practice it ahead of time. Rehearse it with a friend. Be brave. Be bold. Be wonderful you!

You never know what new doors can open for you with an honest, respectful conversation!

Epilogue

I always said, I would do it differently when I was a parent. As a parent of teen daughters, I found myself over-protecting and nagging just like my mother did. Some mothers say, it is a mother's prerogative to worry about her children. But worrying and nagging are not strategies that build the skills a teen needs to be successful in the adult world.

All parents want their children to do better than they have. Even parents in prison wants his or her child to have a better life and stay away from crime.

Parents have two roles, to protect and to guide. By the time you are a teen, their role of protecting you should be near completion. You can feed yourself, dress yourself, go to school and study by yourself. You exercise many choices from your selection of friends to your career path and what classes to take. The parenting role of guide can extend well into adulthood. One of the most effective ways to guide a teen is called modeling. Modeling behavior is part of socializing you, teaching you and equipping you to take your place in the adult world. Letting go of the protection role and the teaching role except by example is one of the hardest tasks a parent undertakes.

I chose to be a mother and was thrilled when I learned I was pregnant. Like most parents, the second I saw my daughter I fell in love. She was born with a birth defect and had to have corrective surgery on the third day of life. It was very scary. I was afraid I might lose her. I had absolutely no control.

All I could do was trust the doctors and pray. Thankfully, she thrived after the second surgery. I learned a very important lesson about parenting early. Parenting is a series of "letting go." From a child's first steps to going to kindergarten, to the first date and going to college. Parenting is a series of opportunities to "let go."

My youngest daughter also had health issues but not until her teen years. It was hard to balance her growing autonomy and guiding her to find the medical, psychological and spiritual resources she needed to get through that crisis. I felt as if I was on a tightrope at times. I needed to be supportive, but I also needed to let go. If the decisions about school and treatment were going to work she needed to buy into them, if not make the decisions for herself. Again, I had to let go. Building trust with communication skills, helped me let go.

I share my parenting journey because I said, I was going to do it differently than my parents. But I found myself worrying and nagging just like my mom. You will never know how hard it is to "let go" until you are a parent. If you have ever suffered from a break up from a boyfriend or girlfriend you have had a little taste of how very hard "letting go" is. When the break up lasts years, like teen and parent, it can be very difficult emotionally. Therefore, I offer the following advice.

Teen to Parent Advise #1) Have **compassion** on your parents because the hardest thing in life is learning to "let go."

Both my daughters, at different times of their lives gave me the most amazing gift. In different ways, in keeping with their own personalities, each of them told me that they received what they needed from me as a parent already. In a way, they let me go. Lovingly they each said, "You've given us all you can mom. I got it from here." Perhaps you can find ways to gently share that truth with your parents. It may take more than once. It may take years. In effect, you are sharing gratitude for all they have given you and asserting yourself by stating you are more independent. However, this statement comes with a double-edged sword, you must also act more independently.